Mountain Biking
the Appalachians

Highlands-Cashiers

ALSO BY LORI FINLEY

Mountain Biking the Appalachians: Brevard-Asheville/The Pisgah Forest

Coming in 1994—
Mountain Biking the Appalachians: Boone-Blowing Rock-Linville

MOUNTAIN BIKING
THE APPALACHIANS

Highlands-Cashiers

by
Lori Finley

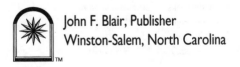
John F. Blair, Publisher
Winston-Salem, North Carolina

BOOK DESIGN BY DEBRA LONG HAMPTON

MAPS BY THE ROBERTS GROUP

PRINTED AND BOUND BY R. R. DONNELLEY & SONS

Library of Congress Cataloging-In-Publication Data

Finley, Lori, 1958–
    Mountain biking the Appalachians. Highlands-Cashiers / by Lori Finley.
        p.   cm.
    Includes index.
    ISBN 0-89587-101-7
    1. Bicycle touring—North Carolina—Nantahala National Forest—Guidebooks.
2. Bicycle touring—South Carolina—Guidebooks.   3. All terrain cycling—North
Carolina—Nantahala National Forest—Guidebooks.   4. All terrain cycling—South
Carolina—Guidebooks.   5. Nantahala National Forest (N.C.)—Guidebooks.   6.
South Carolina—Guidebooks.   I. Title.
GV1045.5.N752N364   1993
796.6'4'097569—dc20   93–17181

For my husband, Bob,
who gave me my first
mountain bike before I
knew I even wanted one

Contents

Horsepasture Area

Acknowledgments

My sincere thanks go to my many friends who helped with the research and production of this book. Two very special friends, Herb Clark and Fred Thomas, were especially generous with their time and their willingness to explore and ride. Most of the time, it was fun and the riding was good, but there were days when nothing seemed to go right. There were occasions when we searched in vain for a trail which, though clearly marked on a map, had long since been consumed by undergrowth; occasions when, deep in the forest, blue winter skies turned on us and began spitting sleet and snow; occasions when a 10-mile ride turned into a 20-mile ride; occasions when we ran out of water and fig bars. Despite these rough days, they always agreed to head to the hills with me again, and for that I am most appreciative.

Others who pedaled along as I researched the trails for this book and who deserve a word of thanks are Sandra Thomas, Steve White, Megan the Wonder Dog, Miller Putnam, Tate Putnam, Billy Enloe, Lewis Lyda, and Andy Baird.

Thanks go to Ed Erwin, Jason Walker, and Bill Mesmer for ride suggestions.

Thanks go to Jim Magruder for sharing his extensive computer know-how in the final production of this manuscript. I also want to thank him for being such a good friend to refrain from laughing when my IQ plummeted to that of a bright-eyed hamster each time my computer screen lit up.

Thanks go to Skip Snow and Boney at Sunshine Cycle Shop for keeping my wheels spinning.

Thanks go to Leroy Howard—there are no words to describe just how much he helped me with this book.

Thanks go to Angie and Roy Costner for assuming the role of surrogate parents while I was on the road.

Thanks go to my precious daughters, Erin and Elizabeth, who tell their friends that the greatest thing about having a writer mom is that she doesn't have the time to take the Christmas tree down until February.

And finally, thanks go to my husband, Bob, for loving me, supporting me, and keeping me humble.

Introduction

Nantahala National Forest is lauded for its hundreds of cascading waterfalls, towering mountains, precipitous gorges, shimmering lakes, and churning whitewater rivers. This national forest, North Carolina's largest at over 500,000 acres, is also recognized for its wealth of mountain-bike routes. Superb single-track trails climb to bald mountain summits, wind into and out of sparkling lakeside coves, plunge through cold mountain creeks, and roll through sunny meadows strewn with colorful wildflowers. These trails, combined with the myriad of dirt roads and gated forest-service roads, offer seemingly endless possibilities for cyclists.

In the 1800s, this area was home to the Cherokee Indians, who are credited with naming it Nantahala, meaning "Land of the Noonday Sun." It is an appropriate name for an area of deep gorges and thundering whitewater rivers that only receive the sun's direct rays at midday.

The Tsali Recreation Area, located near the Nantahala Gorge, also has a strong Cherokee heritage. Considered one of the best mountain-biking areas in the United States, it is named for a Cherokee Indian who escaped with his family from the Trail of Tears to seek refuge in the mountains. Shortly thereafter, Tsali was accused of accidentally killing a United States Army soldier. In exchange for Tsali's surrender, General Winfield Scott promised that the estimated 1,000 Cherokee who had fled from the forced march to Oklahoma would be allowed to remain in the mountains. Tsali requested that he be executed by his own people; he, his oldest son, and his son-in-law were subsequently shot by a Cherokee firing squad near the Tuckasegee River. General Scott kept his promise, and the remaining Indians established the Qualla Indian Reservation in this area. Artifacts of Indian life are still being discovered in the Tsali Recreation Area.

Today, this well-maintained network of trails in the Tsali Recreation Area is used predominantly by horseback riders and mountain bikers. There are three loops which total about 35 miles; all offer great views, abundant creek crossings, and premier single-track riding.

The Nantahala Gorge does not have a monopoly on mountain biking, however. There are excellent rides in and around the Highlands/Cashiers area, along the Chattooga River, and in the Horsepasture area of upstate South Carolina. The heritage of the Cherokee people extends into these regions as well. For example, the Horsepasture area boasts Indian names such as Jocassee, Toxaway, and Oconee, along with an abundance of historical lore.

The routes described in this guide are given a subjective difficulty rating based on length, elevation changes, and trail condition. Some of the rides wind through areas rich in history, some lead past memorable panoramic overlooks, and some are just plain fun to cycle. Whatever your skill level, from beginner to expert, you are sure to agree that this section of the southern Appalachians is a great place to mountain bike.

Planning a Trip

Location

The majority of the rides featured in this guide lie within the boundaries of Nantahala National Forest, which is located in southwestern North Carolina; some rides venture into upstate South Carolina.

Routes

The routes are grouped into regions based on their location. Many of these rides are full-day mountain-bike excursions, while others may take only an hour or two to complete.

Seasons

The winters in western North Carolina are quite mild, so most of these rides can be ridden year-round. Occasionally, winter storms blanket the trails with a light dusting of snow or a little ice, but heavy snowfalls are rare. Some trails require river crossings and should be avoided during cold temperatures due to the risk of hypothermia; these special considerations are noted in the individual ride descriptions. Almost all single-track trails should be avoided after heavy rains because of potential damage from mountain-bike tires; besides, riding soggy trails is just a miserable, muddy experience. Mountain showers can be expected almost every day during the summer months and are often a welcome, cooling relief from the heat. Hunting is permitted in many areas of the forest; mountain bikers are advised to wear fluorescent orange or some other bright, unnatural color.

Equipment and Essentials

Bicycle

A mountain bike or all-terrain bicycle with fat tires is necessary.

Cyclocomputer

A cyclocomputer will make the directions in this book easier to follow, as turns and special features are noted to the tenth of a mile. You can complete these trips without a cyclocomputer, but the chances of getting lost or missing a side trail to a waterfall or other highlight will be increased. Variations in tire pressure, tire size, cyclists' weight, and individual cyclocomputers can produce different mileage readings over identical paths; your readings may not always agree with those provided in this book, but they should be close.

Tool Kit

Many of these trails wind through secluded, remote areas of forest, so a tool kit is highly recommended. Be certain you have a bicycle pump and a patch kit or a spare tube with you; thorns and briers on the trail have flattened many a bicycle tire. If you have never changed a flat tire, learn how and practice at home before you ride.

First-aid Kit

Again, many of these trails are in remote sections of forest where the rescue index is poor. Bring a small, well-appointed first-aid kit with you. It is also a good idea to include a stubby candle and matches in the kit. In winter, you would not want to leave an injured rider without a warming fire while you sought medical assistance.

Water

The creeks and rivers may look pristine, but the days when people could dip their water bottles into a cold mountain stream for a refill are gone. There are some bad bugs around, the most notable being giardia. This one-cell organism can wreak havoc in your intestines if allowed to set up residence. Bring your own drinking water.

Safety

The United States Forest Service makes the following recommendations for safety in the back country:

1. Always let someone know where you are going, what route you are taking, when you expect to return, and what to do if you don't.
2. Check the weather forecast. Be prepared with proper clothing and equipment for all potential weather conditions.
3. Don't push yourself beyond your limits.
4. Keep an eye on each other.
5. Plot your progress on a map as you travel. Know where you are at all times.

Etiquette

Mountain bikers are the new kids on the block, or rather the new kids in the woods. We must be cognizant of the rights of others in the forest and treat others with courtesy. It takes only a few discourteous, irresponsible acts of destructive riding to close a trail to mountain bikes permanently. Ride responsibly. The National Off Road Bicycle Association (NORBA) promotes the following guidelines:

1. Yield the right of way to other nonmotorized recreationists. Realize that people judge all cyclists by your actions.

2. Slow down and use caution when approaching or overtaking others, and make your presence known well in advance.
3. Maintain control of your speed at all times, and approach turns in anticipation of someone around the bend.
4. Stay on designated trails to avoid trampling native vegetation, and minimize potential erosion by not using muddy trails or short-cutting switchbacks.
5. Do not disturb wildlife or livestock.
6. Do not litter. Pack out what you pack in, and pack out more than your share whenever possible.
7. Respect public and private property, including trail-use signs and No Trespassing signs; leave gates as you found them.
8. Be self-sufficient, and let your destination and speed be determined by your ability, your equipment, the terrain, and present and potential weather conditions.
9. Do not travel solo when "bikepacking" in remote areas. Leave word of your destination and when you plan to return.
10. Observe the practice of minimum-impact bicycling by "taking only pictures and memories and leaving only waffle prints."
11. Always wear a helmet whenever you ride.

Many of the trails covered in this guide are also used by equestrians, so exercise courtesy when you encounter horses. Always dismount and give the horse the right of way. If you approach the horse from the front, dismount and stand on the side of the trail. Stay in the horse's line of vision; wait to remount until it has moved well away. If you approach a horse from the rear, dismount and walk slowly until the rider notices you. The rider should move off the trail to allow you to walk your bike past. Remount when you are well away from the horse. If the rider doesn't move off the trail, ask him how he would like you to pass so that you won't spook his horse.

Campgrounds and Overnight Accommodations

Nantahala Gorge Area

The following campgrounds are managed by the Cheoah Ranger District of Nantahala National Forest:

1. Tsali Campground
2. Appletree Campground

For information on these campgrounds, contact

United States Forest Service
Cheoah Ranger District
Route 1, Box 16-A
Robbinsville, N.C. 28771
(704) 479-6431

The following campgrounds, cabins, and motels are privately managed:

1. Lost Mine Campground (704) 488-6445
2. Turkey Creek Campground (704) 488-8966
3. Nantahala Village (704) 488-2826 or (800) 438-1507
4. Nantahala Outdoor Center (704) 488-2175 or (800) 232-7238
5. Freeman's Cabins and Motel (704) 488-2737

For more information on motels and inns in nearby Bryson City, contact the Bryson City Chamber of Commerce at (704) 488-3681.

Highlands/Cashiers Area

The following campgrounds are managed by the Highlands Ranger District of Nantahala National Forest:

1. Vanhook Glade Campground
2. Cliffside Campground

3. Blue Valley Campground (primitive)
4. Ammons Branch Campground (primitive)

For more information on these campgrounds, contact

United States Forest Service
Highlands Ranger District
Route 2, Box 385
Highlands, N.C. 28741
(704) 526-3765

For information on privately managed campgrounds, motels, and inns in the area, contact the Highlands Chamber of Commerce at (704) 526-2112 or the Cashiers Chamber of Commerce at (704) 743-5191.

Horsepasture Area

The following campgrounds are managed by the Andrews Pickens Ranger District of Sumter National Forest:

1. Burrells Ford Campground
2. Cherry Hill Campground

For information on these campgrounds, contact

United States Forest Service
Andrews Pickens Ranger District
Star Route
Walhalla, S.C. 29691
(803) 638-9568

For information on privately managed campgrounds, motels, and inns in this area, contact the Rosman Chamber of Commerce at (704) 883-3700 or the Walhalla Chamber of Commerce at (803) 638-2727.

And when the maps in my mind's eye
fray at the folds and fall to tatters
and trails and tracks combine and collapse
resolve and dissolve in a dream terrain;
then I shall recall all this—
this pastime and my companions,
we went in motion through the light
and seasons seemed to smile on us.

Joel McCollough

Nantahala Gorge Area

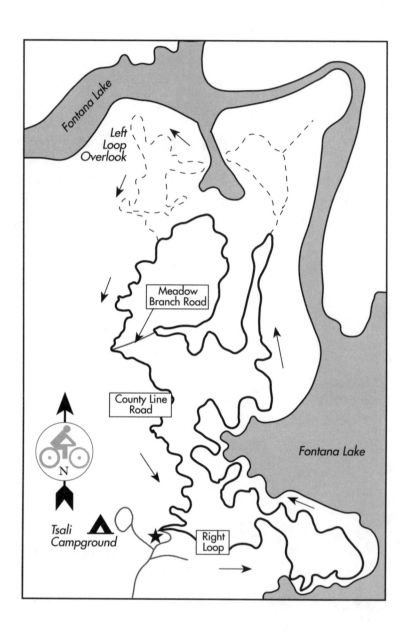

Tsali Trail, Right Loop

Distance: 13.6 miles

Difficulty: Moderate

Riding surface: Single-track trail, gravel road

Map: USGS 7.5 minute quadrangle, Noland Creek

Access: From the junction of U.S. 19/74 and N.C. 28, drive north toward Fontana on N.C. 28 for 3.5 miles. The Tsali Recreation Area is on the right and is marked by a forest-service sign; turn right here. Continue driving for 1.6 miles to an intersection. A right turn will lead you to the boat ramp on Fontana Lake, a left turn will lead you to the campground, and continuing straight will lead you to the parking area for the Left Loop and Right Loop of the Tsali Trail system. Continue straight on F.R. 2250 for 0.2 mile to the trailhead parking area.

Elevation change: The ride begins at an elevation of about 1,850 feet and drops to about 1,725 feet as it winds around the shoreline of Fontana Lake. It climbs to a maximum elevation of about 2,000 feet, then drops back down to 1,850 feet at the parking lot. The total elevation gain is about 275 feet.

Configuration: Loop

*View of Fontana Lake and Great Smoky Mountains
from the Tsali Overlook*

If you could look up the word *paradise* in a mountain biker's thesaurus, you might find synonyms such as *heaven, utopia, Shangri-la,* and *Tsali.* The Tsali Recreation Area has gained national notoriety for its excellent mountain biking and is a resounding favorite of cyclists.

The first time I cycled the Tsali trails, I wondered if I would find the area deserving of all the hype. Mountain-biking tales can be remarkably similar to fishing stories—the same thread of exaggeration seems to be woven through both.

I began by following a trail which meandered through an open stand of pine trees and then plunged through a dark green tunnel of mountain laurel. There were no downed logs lying across the trail, no vertical ascents to push up, no stretches of trail so rocky that my eyeballs were in jeopardy of being jostled out of socket. There was only a picturesque labyrinth of trails climbing mountain ridge lines and then spilling into wildflower-strewn meadows. After only a few miles, I realized that the testimonials were true—this was mountain biking at its best.

The Tsali Trail system is certainly worthy of its reputation as one of the top areas in the United States to mountain bike. Gently rolling terrain dips and curves down to some of the 40-odd coves dotting the shores of Fontana Lake. Challenging in spots, trails ascend up bony, technical ridges to overlooks high above the lake, affording riders spectacular vistas of the nearby Great Smoky Mountains. Plunging downhills, with wilderness flying by and blasts of wind stinging the eyes, evoke the same euphoric thrills as a roller-coaster ride.

There are currently three loops for mountain biking: the Left Loop, the Right Loop, and Thompson's Loop. Because this area is heavily used by both cyclists and horseback riders, the forest service has begun alternating use of the Left and Right loops to separate the two groups. If you are determined to cycle a particular loop, check with the Cheoah Ranger District to be certain the trail will be open to mountain bikes that day.

Tsali's Right Loop begins from the parking lot with a brief climb which soon changes to a gentle descent as it winds toward the banks of Fontana Lake. For the first few miles, you will find yourself traveling at a brisk pace through a hardwood forest with very little understory. This open forest allows good views of shimmering water as the trail follows softly curving contour lines along the many coves that border the lake.

After several miles, the trail turns inland and begins climbing away from the water. It inches up a dusty ridge, winds through a grassy meadow, and then plunges down a rocky, technical descent before intersecting with the trail to the overlook above the lake. The ride then continues on a narrow descending trail. There are several creek crossings flanked by typical creek-side flora: lacy hemlock, deep green rhododendron, and seasonal wildflowers such as bluets, violets, orchids, wild phlox, and foxglove.

The second overlook, which is shared by the Left Loop, offers the most spectacular views of any on the ride. During autumn, when the hardwoods are dressed in their most splendid colors, a mountain-bike ride up to this overlook is especially rewarding. The vibrant contrast of the deep blue water against the glowing reds, oranges, and yellows of the changing leaves is exceptionally beautiful. This spot is an ideal place to enjoy a snack before descending to the next intersection.

Then comes a final, grueling ascent that will get your heart rate up in a hurry. This dirt road intersects with County Line Road on the edge of a sun-glazed meadow; this final leg of the loop leads back to the parking lot.

Vivid orange blossoms of flame azaleas along the Right Loop of the Tsali Trail

0.0 From the parking lot, take the trail on the right. You will need to start in low gear, since the trail begins on a brief climb.

2.8 You will come to a fork in the trail. Take the right fork and begin a technical descent. (The left fork leads to County Line Road and the parking lot.)

5.7 You will arrive at an intersection of trails. This ride continues straight to the overlook. (If you choose not to cycle to the overlook, make a sharp left turn. Note: This will shorten the ride by 1.5 miles.)

6.4 You will arrive at the overlook. To continue the ride, retrace your route to the intersection of trails.

7.2 Bear right at the intersection.

7.7 There is a grass road to the left which leads to County Line Road. Continue straight.

8.2 Turn right.

9.8 County Line Road is to the left. The trail leading to the Left Loop Overlook is to the right. Turn right and begin the steep, technical climb to the overlook. (Note: If you choose not to ride to the overlook, the loop will be shortened by 1.3 miles.)

10.6 You will arrive at the overlook. There are dangerous, sheer drop-offs, so stay away from the edge. To continue the ride, cycle straight on the trail past the overlook. You will come to a sharp, very steep switchback on the left almost immediately; be sure to anticipate this switchback.

11.1 You will come to an intersection of trails. Take the trail to the left, which leads to County Line Road. Prepare yourself for the serious climb ahead.

11.7 Turn left onto County Line Road.

12.4 Meadow Branch Road enters from the left. Continue straight on County Line Road back to the parking lot.

13.6 Cycle around the steel gate which marks the end of the ride.

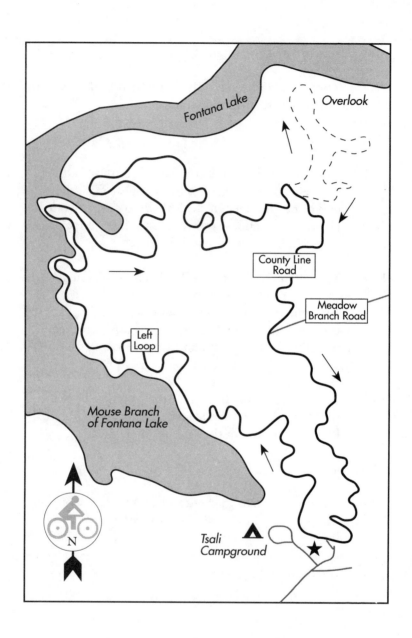

Fontana Lake

Overlook

County Line Road

Meadow Branch Road

Left Loop

Mouse Branch of Fontana Lake

N

Tsali Campground

Tsali Trail, Left Loop

Distance: 11 miles

Difficulty: Moderate

Riding surface: Single-track trail, gravel road

Map: USGS 7.5 minute quadrangle, Noland Creek

Access: From the junction of U.S. 19/74 and N.C. 28, drive north toward Fontana on N.C. 28 for 3.5 miles. The Tsali Recreation Area is on the right and is marked by a forest-service sign; turn right here. Continue driving for 1.6 miles to an intersection. A right turn will lead you to the boat ramp on Fontana Lake, a left turn will lead you to the campground, and continuing straight will lead you to the parking area for the Left Loop and Right Loop of the Tsali Trail system. Continue straight on F.R. 2250 for 0.2 mile to the trailhead parking area.

Elevation change: The ride begins at an elevation of about 1,850 feet and drops to a minimum of about 1,725 feet as it winds among the coves of Mouse Branch of Fontana Lake. It climbs to a maximum elevation of about 2,000 feet, then drops back to 1,850 feet at the parking lot. The total elevation gain is about 275 feet.

Configuration: Loop

Stopping to rest in a meadow along the Tsali Trail

Tsali's Left Loop begins as a narrow, rolling trail which descends to skirt the banks of Mouse Branch of Fontana Lake. The trail meanders along the contour lines through a hardwood forest whose flora is typical of the lower slopes of the Appalachians. This is an open, wooded area with little understory, offering good views of the azure waters of Fontana Lake during the first few miles of riding.

In addition to the vistas across the lake, there are several other highlights during the first part of the ride. At the 1-mile mark, there is an old stone chimney standing beside the trail; you will ride directly through what was probably the kitchen of an early settler's home. There are also a number of ridable creek crossings which are fringed with wildflowers in the late spring and summer.

The trail begins a mild ascent, reaching heights of several hundred feet above Fontana Lake. It is quite narrow, off-camber, technical, and even dangerous in spots. There is one especially tricky rocky section that barely hangs onto the edge of a precipitous cliff; this spot is potentially dangerous if not negotiated cautiously. There are also several sections that have gnarled, twisted "tombstone" roots that can dismount careless riders. This rough section is very brief.

As the trail leads away from the water, it begins a fairly serious climb through a hardwood forest. It then descends to a low-lying area which has one treacherous creek crossing. A climb up to the overlook provides a fantastic view of the Great Smoky Mountains and Fontana Lake. This spot, with its unsurpassed scenery, makes an ideal place to rest.

The last climb of the ride is on a bony, technical dirt road which leads to County Line Road. Just when you think you can't go any farther, the road ends at a T-intersection on the edge of a beautiful, flat meadow. The thrilling descent that follows will make you feel like you are riding on the wings of the wind.

0.0　From the parking lot, take the left trail, which descends toward the lake.

1.0　There is an old stone chimney standing off to the right.

6.2　The trail curves sharply to the right; there are exposed roots in this section which should be approached cautiously.

7.6　You will arrive at an intersection of trails. Bear to the left to cycle up to the overlook. (A right turn will take you to County Line Road, which leads back to the parking lot. The ride will be shortened by 1 mile if you do not ride to the overlook.)

8.1　You will arrive at the overlook. There are excellent views of Fontana Lake and the Great Smoky Mountains. There are also sheer, dangerous drop-offs, so stay away from the edge of the cliff. To continue the ride, backtrack toward the intersection of trails.

Cycling along Fontana Lake on the Left Loop of the Tsali Trail

8.2   There is a very sharp switchback on the left; you should anticipate this switchback and negotiate it with caution.

8.6   You will arrive at an intersection with the Left Loop; continue straight toward County Line Road.

8.7   You will arrive at an intersection with the Right Loop; follow the trail on the right, which is marked "To County Line Road." You will begin a steep climb.

9.2   Turn left onto County Line Road. Straight ahead is a meadow.

9.9   County Line Road intersects with Meadow Branch Road, which enters on the left. Continue straight.

11.0   You will arrive back at the parking lot.

Chimney near the Left Loop of the Tsali Trail

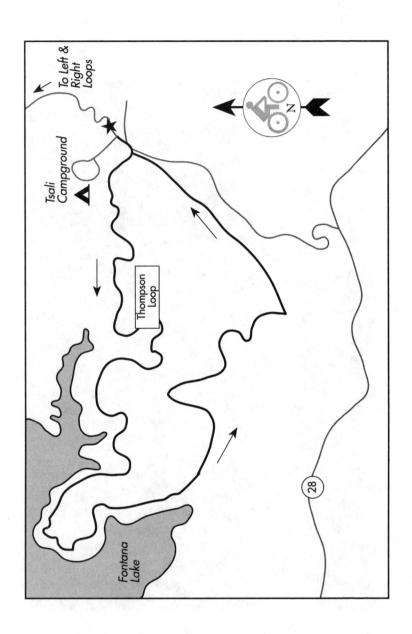

To Left & Right Loops

Tsali Campground

Thompson Loop

Fontana Lake

28

N

Tsali Trail, Thompson Loop

Distance: 7.4 miles

Difficulty: Moderate to easy

Riding surface: Single-track trail

Map: USGS 7.5 minute quadrangle, Noland Creek

Access: From the junction of U.S. 19/74 and N.C. 28, drive north toward Fontana on N.C. 28 for 3.5 miles. The Tsali Recreation Area is on the right and is marked by a forest-service sign; turn right here. Continue driving for 1.6 miles to an intersection. Park in the parking area across from the Thompson Loop trailhead. (The left road leads to the camp-ground, the right road leads to the Fontana Lake boat ramp, and the road straight ahead leads to the parking area for the Left Loop and Right Loop of the Tsali Trail system.)

Elevation change: The ride begins at an elevation of about 1,750 feet and gradually climbs to a maximum of about 2,050 feet. It then descends back to 1,750 feet at the parking lot. The total elevation gain is about 300 feet.

Configuration: Loop

Thompson Loop, which opened to cyclists in 1992, is the newest, shortest, and easiest of the three loops currently available for mountain biking in the Tsali Recreation Area. This trail is dedicated to the memory of David Thompson, a former wilderness ranger of the Cheoah Ranger District. There is a wooden sign at one of the highest points on the trail commemorating Thompson and his work.

The trail begins on a wide, old logging road which leads through a dark, dense hardwood forest. After about 0.5 mile, you will turn left onto a rolling single-track trail which meanders along the banks of Fontana Lake. This section of the ride is spiced with several creek crossings and lush, deep green rhododendron.

You will then leave the water's edge and begin a gradual climb up the ridge. The ride continues with a left turn onto an open logging road which is often hot and dusty during the dog days of summer. The ride culminates in a screaming downhill which offers exceptional views of Fontana Lake and the surrounding mountains. But you may never notice these views; your attention will probably be focused on your rapidly increasing speed and flashes of trail railing underfoot. Reality is just around the

Cycling through an open section of Thompson Loop of the Tsali Trail

Fast, fun section of Thompson Loop of the Tsali Trail

bend, though, and as you reluctantly tap the brakes, you might find yourself thinking that this is as close to nirvana as you will ever get.

0.0   The trail begins beyond the gated road to the left of the Tsali campground road.

0.7   A grassy logging road climbs a hill on the right. Bear left to stay on Thompson Loop.

4.6   The majority of the climbing is now over. The trail enters an old roadbed.

6.1   The trail comes to a T-intersection with a logging road; Thompson Loop continues to the left for a short climb.

7.3   This leg of Thompson Loop empties into the first part of the loop; bear right toward the parking area.

7.4   You will arrive back at the parking area.

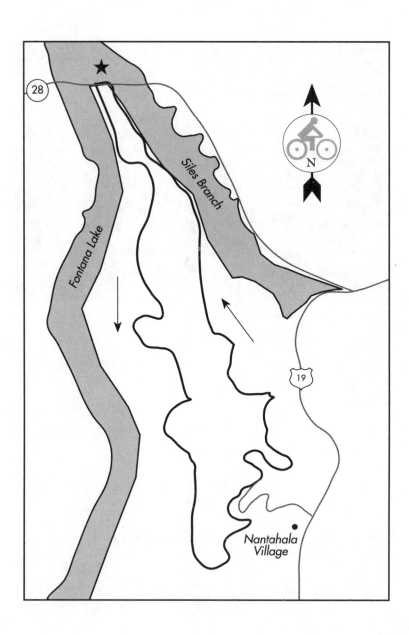

Knobscorcher Trail Loop

Distance: 3.7 miles

Difficulty: Moderate

Riding surface: Single-track trail, dirt road

Map: USGS 7.5 minute quadrangle, Wesser

Access: From the junction of U.S. 19/74 and N.C. 28, drive north toward Fontana on N.C. 28 for 1 mile to the bridge. Park at one of the pull-offs on the south side of the bridge.

Elevation change: The ride begins at an elevation of 1,700 feet on N.C. 28 and climbs to a maximum of 1,950 feet at about the halfway point. The total elevation gain is 250 feet.

Configuration: Loop

Cycling along a level section of Knobscorcher Trail

I f you like thrills, you will love Knobscorcher Trail. Nestled at the foot of the Great Smoky Mountains, this short ride will really test your technical skills.

The trail begins along the shores of Fontana Lake and quickly gains altitude as it scratches its way up the side of a ridge. It periodically winds through openings in the woods overlooking the surrounding mountains and water. There are several descents on steep sections of trail that require advanced technical skills and are certain to quicken your pulse.

This loop of trails has recently been the race site for the Knobscorcher Mountain Bike Festival, which is held several times a year. Area cyclists use this loop for building and fine-tuning technical skills. Don't let the length fool you into thinking this is an easy ride; this loop can be made into a strenuous workout if ridden several times in succession.

0.0 From the parking pull-off on N.C. 28, begin on the left side of the road next to the bridge over Fontana Lake. Turn left and cycle up the hill. The loop begins on a gated logging road. Fontana Lake will be on your right as you start the ride.

0.1 Turn left off this level trail. You will cycle up a steep hill; dismounting may be necessary.

0.8 You will come to a fork in the trail; take the fork to the right. You will begin a dangerously steep, technical descent. Negotiate this section cautiously. At the end of the descent, continue straight on the wide logging road.

1.0 You will come to a fork where a trail enters the logging road. Bear right around the bend.

1.2 A nice view of Fontana Lake and the Great Smoky Mountains is to the right.

1.5 Make a hard right turn. Continue on a descending grade.

1.6   Turn left onto the grass road.

1.7   There is an intersection of trails; continue straight up the hill.

1.9   Turn left onto a dirt road after passing a house.

2.0   Bear left around the bend.

2.2   You will reach a paved road. Turn left to continue the loop. (A right turn leads to the Nantahala Village Inn and Restaurant.)

2.4   Bear left off the paved road and push your bike up the steep single-track trail.

2.8   Bear left at the fork in the trail. You will descend a steep, technical trail which should be negotiated with extreme caution.

3.1   The trail ends at an intersection with a narrow, paved road at the edge of Fontana Lake. Turn left to complete the loop.

3.7   The narrow, paved road ends at N.C. 28. Cycle back to your parked vehicle.

Pausing to rest along Knobscorcher Trail

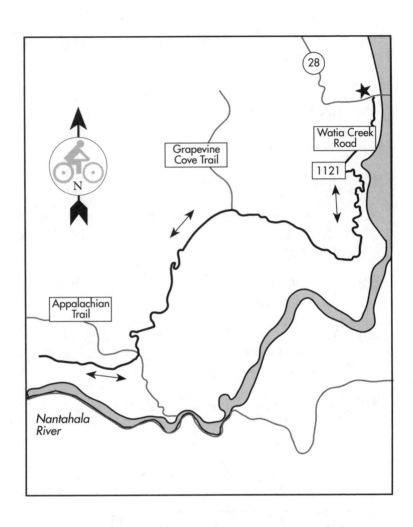

28

Watia Creek
Road

1121

Grapevine
Cove Trail

Appalachian
Trail

Nantahala
River

N

Watia Creek Road Ride

Distance: 13.6 Miles

Difficulty: Moderate

Riding surface: Dirt and gravel roads

Map: USGS 7.5 minute quadrangle, Wesser

Access: From the junction of U.S. 19/74 and N.C. 28, drive north toward Fontana on N.C. 28 for 1 mile to the bridge over Fontana Lake. Park at one of the pull-offs on the north side of the bridge. The ride follows Watia Creek Road (F.R. 1121), which begins north of the bridge on the left side of N.C. 28.

Elevation change: The ride begins on N.C. 28 at an elevation of 1,700 feet. It climbs to 2,000 feet, only to drop to 1,800 feet in the first few miles. It again climbs to 2,000 feet at the Grapevine Cove trailhead, then ascends to 2,400 feet at the intersection with the Appalachian Trail, finally reaching a maximum of 2,600 feet at the end of the forest-service road. The total elevation gain is 1,100 feet.

Configuration: Out and back

Watia Creek Road winds past mountain farms

Watia Creek Road winds through the Nantahala National Forest on a gradually climbing grade. It offers mountain bikers a good workout, as well as one of the best views of the Nantahala Gorge in the area. The gorge, whose precipitous walls rise close to 2,000 feet in sections, runs for about 8 miles from Aquone Lake, the highest lake in North Carolina, to Wesser.

The Nantahala River, which thunders through the gorge, is the most popular whitewater river in North Carolina. Its waters are piped over the mountains from Aquone Lake to the power plant just upstream of the boaters' put-in.

Nantahala is the Cherokee word for "Land of the Noonday Sun." It seems an appropriate name for this gorge, whose towering walls admit only a few hours of sunshine each day. The water temperature averages only 45 to 50 degrees year-round as the river cuts a churning, shivering path through the scenic gorge on its way to Fontana Lake. During the warm summer months, early-morning fog often hangs over the river because of the cold water temperature. Visibility often drops to only a few feet, thereby creating an eerie feeling for the shrouded paddler blindly approaching the roaring rapids.

This ride begins on a gravel road near Almond and parallels Fontana Lake for a short distance. It then climbs away from the lake while paralleling Watia Creek on its way through Hickory Cove. Before reaching the Grapevine Cove trailhead, you will pass several modest mountain homes complete with protective dogs, which presumably boast sharp teeth. Watia Creek Road crosses the Appalachian Trail just before reaching a dead end on the edge of the Nantahala Gorge. You will then retrace your path and descend back to N.C. 28.

0.0   Turn left off N.C. 28 onto Watia Creek Road.

3.5   The Grapevine Cove trailhead is on the right.

5.6   Watia Creek Road crosses the Appalachian Trail.

5.7   You will come to a fork in the road; take the right fork and cycle around the gate across the road.

6.8   The road ends. Turn around and retrace your path down to N.C. 28.

13.6   You will reach the intersection with N.C. 28.

Plunging through a creek on Grapevine Cove Trail

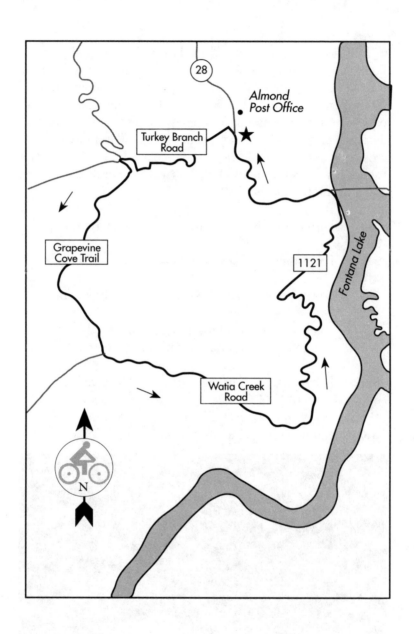

28

Almond
Post Office

Turkey Branch
Road

Grapevine
Cove Trail

1121

Fontana Lake

Watia Creek
Road

N

Turkey Branch Road / Grapevine Cove Trail / Watia Creek Road Loop

Distance: 7 miles

Difficulty: Moderate

Riding surface: Single-track trail, dirt and gravel roads

Maps: 1. USGS 7.5 minute quadrangle, Noland Creek
2. USGS 7.5 minute quadrangle, Wesser

Access: From the junction of U.S. 19/74 and N.C. 28, drive north toward Fontana on N.C. 28 for 1.9 miles to the Almond post office, which will be on your right. On weekends, when the post office is closed, park here; ask for permission to park during business hours.

Elevation change: The ride begins at an elevation of about 1,900 feet at the Almond post office. At the 1-mile mark, the trail reaches 2,500 feet. The elevation drops on Grapevine Cove Trail, eventually reaching a minimum of 1,700 feet at the junction of Watia Creek Road (F.R. 1121) and N.C. 28. One last brief climb to the Almond post office will bring you back to an elevation of 1,900 feet. The total elevation gain is 800 feet.

Configuration: Loop

View of Fontana Lake and the surrounding Great Smoky Mountains from Turkey Branch Road

This loop packs a lot of punch in just 7 miles of trail. Beautiful scenery, outstanding views, technical single-track riding, countless "whoop-de-dos," granny-gear climbs, and wild descents are some of the highlights you will encounter.

The loop begins on Turkey Branch Road, which climbs a steep grade for 1.5 miles through rich, dark green rhododendron and past trickling streams. Several panoramic vistas of the Great Smoky Mountains and Fontana Lake provide a great excuse to stop and rest.

The ride begins a fast descent on Grapevine Cove Trail, which plunges through a mixed-hardwood forest. There are dozens of moguls that will have you catching air and hollering "Yee-ha!" There are so many, though, that jumping them can become monotonous. Cycling these whoop-de-dos tends to induce an anesthetized state which can make cyclists a little sloppy. On one occasion, after cycling mogul after mogul, I found myself careening off the trail in a dazed stupor. Though I wasn't hurt, I must have been an amusing sight when I finally staggered out of the woods with tree branches sticking out of my helmet like deer antlers.

You will leave the single-track and turn left onto Watia Creek

Road, a gravel road which leads past a number of small mountain homes; several resident dogs with glistening incisors are certain to come out on the road to greet you. I've found that a loud yell and a squirt from my water bottle generally keep them from getting too close.

The ride ends with a left turn onto N.C. 28 and a short climb back to the post office.

0.0   Cross N.C. 28 and cycle down the gravel road which begins directly across from the post office.

0.9   There is a great view of Fontana Lake and the Great Smoky Mountains on the right.

1.0   A small cascading stream is on the right. You will come to a fork in the road; take the road to the left, which continues past an old steel gate.

1.4   You will come to a junction of three trails. Take the single-track trail on the far left and begin a descent.

1.9   You will come to a creek crossing.

2.3   You will reach another creek crossing.

2.7   The trail ends on a gravel road; turn left.

4.9   There is an excellent view of Fontana Lake and the surrounding Great Smoky Mountains.

6.2   Watia Creek Road ends at the intersection with N.C. 28. Fontana Lake is on the right. Turn left onto N.C. 28 and cycle back to the post office.

7.0   You will arrive back at the Almond post office.

Highlands-Cashiers Area

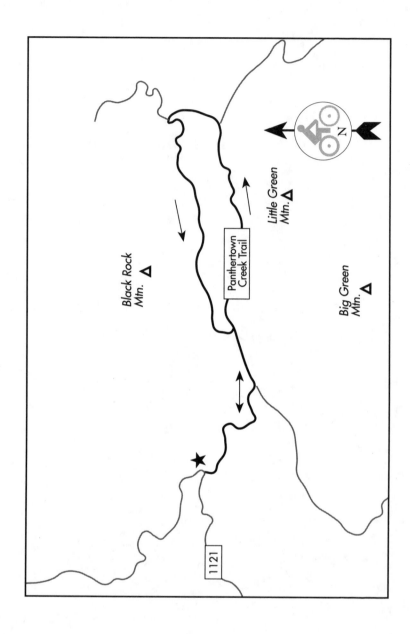

Panthertown Creek Trail Loop

Distance: 4.6 miles

Difficulty: Easy

Riding surface: Dirt road, single-track trail, logging road

Maps: 1. USGS 7.5 minute quadrangle, Big Ridge
2. Nantahala National Forest Map

Access: From Cashiers, take U.S. 64 East. Drive approximately 2 miles, then turn left (north) onto Cedar Creek Road (S.R. 1120). Follow this road for 1.7 miles. Turn right onto Breedlove Road (S.R. 1121) and continue for 3.6 miles to the parking area at the end of the road. The national-forest boundary is here.

Elevation change: The ride begins at an elevation of 4,100 feet at the parking area. It descends to 3,700 feet at the intersection of trails at 0.9 mile, then drops to 3,650 feet as the trail parallels Panthertown Creek. It climbs to 3,750 feet at the intersection with the grass road, then slowly climbs another 100 feet. You will again descend to 3,700 feet at the intersection of trails before climbing back to 4,100 feet at the parking area. The total elevation gain is about 600 feet.

Configuration: Loop

Cycling along the base of Blackrock Mountain in the Panthertown Valley area

This ride begins on a descending dirt road which features an overlook with excellent views of the Panthertown Valley, Blackrock Mountain, Little Green Mountain, and Boardcamp Ridge. It continues on a level grade as it winds along the banks of Panthertown Creek. Though the trail is easy, a degree of technical skill is necessary in some sandy sections.

The trail is quite scenic as it makes its way among tall hardwood trees, hemlocks, and mountain laurel. There are several ridable creek crossings which add interest. Be sure to notice the old wooden shed that sits on the bank of Panthertown Creek. This shed is located near a large sand bar in the creek which attracts sunbathers and swimmers during the warm summer months.

After a few miles, you will make a left turn onto a grassy logging road which skirts the base of Blackrock Mountain. This road provides a good mix of mild climbs and gentle descents. The last leg of the loop is a significant climb from the valley back up to the parking area. If the climb gets to be too much for the beginners in your group, walk your bikes the rest of the way.

0.0 Cycle around the steel gate and descend on the unmarked service road.

0.3   To the left is a view of the valley and the surrounding mountains.

0.6   There is a dirt road on the right; continue straight.

0.9   You will arrive at an intersection of trails; continue straight.

1.7   The trail passes an old wooden shed that sits near Panthertown Creek.

2.2   There is a grass road on the left; turn left here.

3.6   You will cross the creek on a wooden bridge; continue straight.

3.7   You will arrive at an intersection of trails; turn right and begin the steady climb back to the parking area.

4.6   You will arrive at the parking area.

View of Boardcamp Ridge from the Panthertown Creek Trail Loop

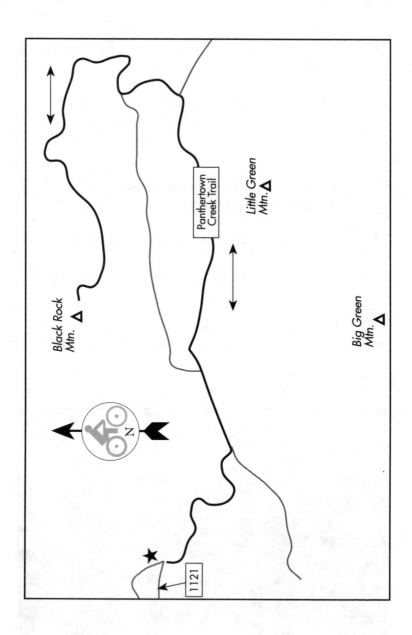

Black Rock
Mtn. △

Panthertown
Creek Trail

Little Green
Mtn. △

Big Green
Mtn. △

N

1121

Blackrock Mountain Ride

Distance: 6.6 miles

Difficulty: Moderate

Riding surface: Dirt road, single-track trail

Maps: 1. USGS 7.5 minute quadrangle, Big Ridge
        2. Nantahala National Forest Map

Access: From Cashiers, take U.S. 64 East. Drive approximately 2 miles, then turn left (north) onto Cedar Creek Road (S.R. 1120). Follow this road for 1.7 miles. Turn right onto Breedlove Road (S.R. 1121) and continue for 3.6 miles to the parking area at the end of the road. The national-forest boundary is here.

Elevation change: The ride begins at an elevation of 4,100 feet at the parking area. It descends to 3,700 feet at the intersection of trails at 0.9 mile, then continues to a minimum of 3,650 feet at the creek. It climbs to 3,750 feet at the grass road, then ascends to 4,400 feet at the summit of Blackrock Mountain. On the return trip, the trail descends to 3,650 feet along Panthertown Creek before climbing back to the parking lot at 4,100 feet. The total elevation gain is 1,200 feet.

Configuration: Out and back

View of the Panthertown Valley from the summit of Blackrock Mountain

This tour meanders up to the summit of Blackrock Mountain, which features one of the best views of Panthertown Valley in the area.

The ride begins with a descent on a scenic dirt road flanked by rhododendron, laurel, and a variety of hardwoods. Sections of this road are heavily canopied with tree branches from the surrounding forest, while other sections are open, sunny, and punctuated with blue skies.

The dirt road leads to a level, sandy single-track trail which winds along the banks of Panthertown Creek. The trail then climbs away from the valley up to the peak of Blackrock Mountain. Toward the top, the route becomes quite technical. Sections of the trail are actually flat, ridable rock. Cyclists should be forewarned that the overlook at the granite peak can be slippery and dangerous when wet or icy.

Enjoy this panoramic overlook before turning around and retracing your path down the mountain.

0.0   Cycle around the gate and begin descending on the dirt road.

0.9   You will come to an intersection of trails; continue straight.

1.8   There is a trail to the right; continue straight.

2.7   You will come to a fork in the trail; take the left fork.

3.0   The trail becomes covered with rock.

3.3   There is short spur trail to the left which will take you to an overlook offering views of the surrounding mountains and the entire valley. To continue the ride, turn around and retrace your path to the parking area.

6.6   You will arrive back at the parking area.

View of Boardcamp Ridge from the Panthertown Valley

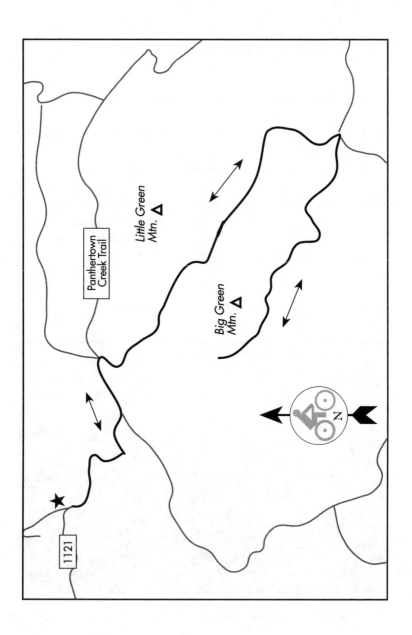

Big Green Mountain Ride

Distance: 7.8 miles

Difficulty: Moderate

Riding surface: Dirt road, single-track trail

Maps: 1. USGS 7.5 minute quadrangle, Big Ridge
2. Nantahala National Forest Map

Access: From Cashiers, take U.S. 64 East. Drive approximately 2 miles, then turn left (north) onto Cedar Creek Road (S.R. 1120). Follow this road for 1.7 miles. Turn right onto Breedlove Road (S.R. 1121) and continue for 3.6 miles to the parking area at the end of the road. The national-forest boundary is here.

Elevation change: The ride begins at an elevation of 4,100 feet at the parking area. It drops to a minimum of 3,650 feet at the Panthertown Creek crossing, then climbs to a maximum of 4,200 feet at the summit of Big Green Mountain. On the return trip, the ride descends back to 3,650 feet at the creek crossing and climbs again to 4,100 feet at the parking area. The total elevation gain is 1,000 feet.

Configuration: Out and back

View of Little Green Mountain from overlook

This tour begins on a descending dirt road which plunges through verdant stands of rhododendron and hardwood trees. There is an overlook on the left from which you can see for miles. It offers outstanding views of the valley below and the surrounding mountains, such as Boardcamp Ridge, Little Green Mountain, and Blackrock Mountain.

At the intersection of trails, you will turn right onto a level single-track trail which bisects the valley lying between Little Green Mountain and Big Green Mountain. Several pretty creek crossings and good campsites are located along this trail. There are also occasional sandy sections which require some technical maneuvering. Leaving the open valley, the trail plunges through a dense pine forest whose floor is carpeted with a prolific ground cover called "turkey feet," which is common in the southern Appalachians.

The trail then begins climbing the eastern ridge of Big Green Mountain. After several miles of gradual climbing, you will reach the summit of this scenic granite bald. The western side of this peak has a sheer drop-off which is camouflaged by evergreen bushes, so exercise caution and stay away from the edge. After resting, retrace your path back down to the valley.

0.0   Begin the ride by cycling around the steel gate and descending on the unmarked service road.

0.3   Panthertown Valley is visible on the left side of the road.

0.6   There is a dirt road on the right; continue straight.

0.9   You will arrive at an intersection of trails; turn right.

1.0   There is a camping area on the left, complete with a brick grill.

1.1   You will cross Panthertown Creek on a rickety wooden bridge.

2.6   You will arrive at an intersection of trails; turn right to continue up Big Green Mountain.

3.8   You will come to a fork in the trail; take the left fork, which leads to the top of the mountain.

3.9   You will arrive at the top of Big Green Mountain. Turn around and begin retracing your path back down.

7.8   You will arrive at the parking area.

Pine-needle laden, single-track trail through a stand of rhododendron

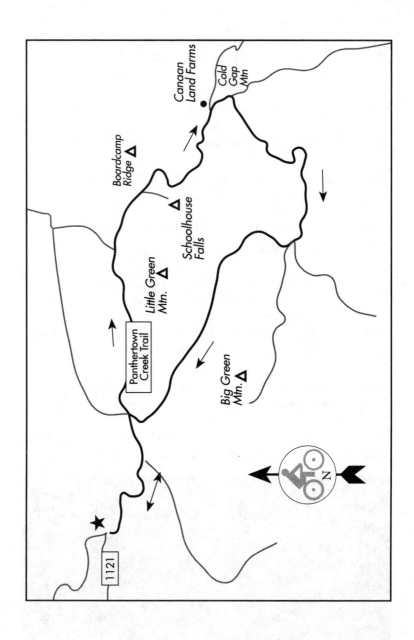

Canaan Land Loop

Distance: 7.5 miles

Difficulty: Moderate

Riding surface: Dirt road, single-track trail

Maps: 1. USGS 7.5 minute quadrangle, Big Ridge
2. USGS 7.5 minute quadrangle, Lake Toxaway
3. Nantahala National Forest Map

Access: From Cashiers, take U.S. 64 East. Drive approximately 2 miles, then turn left (north) onto Cedar Creek Road (S.R. 1120). Follow this road for 1.7 miles. Turn right onto Breedlove Road (S.R. 1121) and continue for 3.6 miles to the parking area at the end of the road. The national-forest boundary is here.

Elevation change: The ride starts at an elevation of 4,100 feet at the parking area. It descends to 3,700 feet in Panthertown Valley and drops another 50 feet by the time it reaches the crossing at Greenland Creek. It then begins a moderate climb toward Canaan Land, which has an elevation of 3,800 feet. You will climb to 3,950 feet on the gravel road and reach 4,000 feet at the intersection of trails at 4.8 miles. The elevation drops to 3,650 feet at Panthertown Creek before climbing back to 4,100 feet at the parking area. The total elevation gain is 800 feet.

Configuration: Loop

This ride, which offers winding dirt roads, scenic single-track trails, and historical landmarks, will award cyclists with a premium mountain-bike ride.

The loop begins on a descending dirt road flanked by a mixed-hardwood forest dotted with dark green mountain laurel and rhododendron. There is a panoramic view of the entire Panthertown Valley and the nearby mountains on the left at about 0.5 mile. At the first intersection of trails, the ride continues straight, winding along the banks of Panthertown Creek before crossing it on a wooden bridge.

The trail then dips and curves along Greenland Creek, crossing it via a second wooden bridge at about 2 miles. Nestled in the laurel just before the bridge is a narrow spur trail which leads to Schoolhouse Falls; this trail is not ridable, but it can be hiked for the short distance to these beautiful falls. Hide your bike in the bushes off the main trail to ward off any would-be thieves.

The ride continues on a climbing road which seems tougher than it actually is because of its loose-gravel surface. After cycling around a steel gate blocking the road, you will see a wooden fence and a sign for Canaan Land Farms; this is private property and should be respected as such. Shortly thereafter, the road passes the main entrance to Canaan Land. This Christian retreat was formerly Camp Toxaway, circa 1920. Prior to that, it was known as the Baccus Lodge, circa 1907. During that period,

Schoolhouse Falls on the Canaan Land Loop

Well-conditioned, single-track trail through the forest

it served as a hunting lodge and retreat for such dignitaries as Thomas Edison and Henry Ford. Be sure to note the plaque near the entrance indicating that this farm is listed on the National Register of Historic Places.

The tour then returns to single-track trail and crosses Greenland Creek, which is quite deep. (Note: This ride should be avoided in cold weather because there is no dry way to cross this creek. Also, during times of high water, the creek may be extremely difficult, if not impossible, to ford safely.)

You will cross another small creek before the trail narrows and squeezes through an extraordinary stand of rhododendron. There are huge, mature bushes as far as the eye can see. In fact, they are so prolific that you may wonder if kudzu is giving the rhododendron private lessons in the art of propagation. During the month of June, when the rhododendron is in full bloom, this section of trail is stunning, with thousands of pink blossoms adorning the shiny, dark green leaves of the bushes.

0.0   From the parking area, cycle around the gate and descend on the dirt road.

0.9 You will come to an intersection of trails; continue straight.

1.8 Bear to the right and cross the wooden bridge over Panthertown Creek.

2.2 You will approach a wooden bridge across Greenland Creek. Just before the bridge, you will see a narrow spur trail nestled in the laurel bushes; this trail leads to Schoolhouse Falls.

2.3 Just past the bridge, there is a logging road on the left; continue straight.

3.0 There is a gate across the road. Continue straight to another gate.

3.1 Continue straight past the second gate. There is a metal bridge across the creek. To the left are a wooden fence and a sign for Canaan Land Farms.

3.3 You will pass the main entrance to Canaan Land. Turn right onto another gravel road.

3.5 There is a gated grass road on the right. Follow the single-track trail that begins on the left side of the gate.

3.6 The trail passes under power lines.

4.2 Turn right and cross Greenland Creek. This is a deep creek which should be avoided during cold weather because of the risk of hypothermia; also, after heavy rains, you may not be able to ford this creek because of its depth and currents. Avoid this loop under such conditions.

4.3 The trail crosses another creek before heading into an extraordinary stand of rhododendron.

4.4 The trail again crosses a creek. There are slick rocks on this crossing, so be very careful. The trail becomes quite narrow and difficult to ride because of rocks and downed limbs.

4.7 Bear left at the fork.

4.8 You will arrive at an intersection of trails. Take the trail on the right and begin a rocky descent.

6.6 You will arrive at another intersection of trails. Turn left to climb back up to the parking area.

7.5 You will arrive at the parking area.

Cycling through Greenland Creek

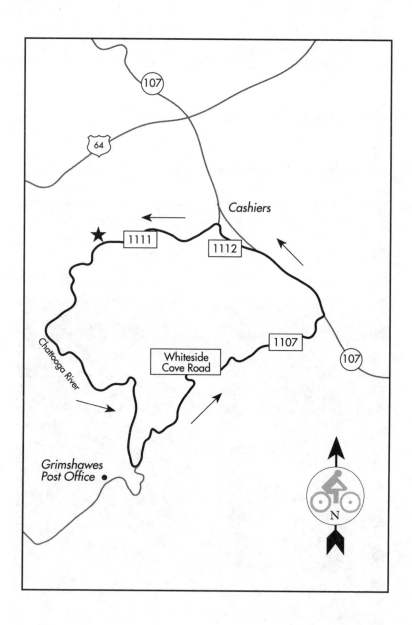

Cashiers Valley /
Timber Ridge Loop

Distance: 8.4 miles

Difficulty: Moderate

Riding surface: Single-track trail, dirt road, paved road

Maps: 1. USGS 7.5 minute quadrangle, Cashiers
2. Nantahala National Forest Map

Access: From the junction of U.S. 64 and N.C. 107 in Cashiers, head south on N.C. 107 for 0.5 mile. Turn right onto F.R. 1112 and proceed 0.2 mile. Turn right onto F.R. 1111, which is the second road on the right. Drive 1.1 miles and park at the end of the road.

Elevation change: The ride begins at an elevation of 3,400 feet at the parking area, then drops to a minimum of 3,000 feet at the intersection with Whiteside Cove Road. It climbs back to 3,400 feet before dropping to 3,300 feet at the intersection with N.C. 107. You will gain a final 100 feet of elevation on the ride back to the parking area. The total elevation gain is 500 feet.

Configuration: Loop

Level, single-track trail through lush stand of rhododendron

This loop begins on a descending single-track trail which plunges through a hardwood forest draped with gnarled grapevines. After about 1 mile, the trail enters a mature pine forest. It continues on its winding course along the western base of Timber Ridge before spilling into the Chattooga River. The river must be forded at this point. (Note: This loop should be avoided during cold weather due to the risk of hypothermia. The river should also be avoided after heavy rains because it is difficult, if not impossible, to cross at high water.)

The ride continues on a single-track trail until ending at Whiteside Cove Road just above the Grimshawes post office. A left turn onto this scenic, ascending paved road will lead you back to N.C. 107 and ultimately to the starting point.

0.0 From the parking area, take the trail on the left and begin descending.

0.6 There is an intersection of trails; continue straight. (Note: You can turn left here for an optional excursion to the rapids on the Chattooga River. The trail ends after 0.5 mile; from there, you can hike to the edge of the river. Taking this optional leg will add 1 mile to the ride.)

0.8   There is a fork in the trail; continue straight.

0.9   The trail crosses the Chattooga River and continues almost directly across the stream.

1.7   The trail makes a T-intersection with a logging road. Turn left to continue.

3.7   Turn left onto Whiteside Cove Road.

4.1   Norton Cemetery is on the right; continue straight.

6.0   You will come to an intersection with N.C. 107. Turn left to continue.

7.2   Turn left onto F.R. 1112.

7.3   Turn right onto F.R. 1111.

8.4   You will arrive back at your vehicle.

Cashiers Valley Tour winding through a forest draped with curving grapevines

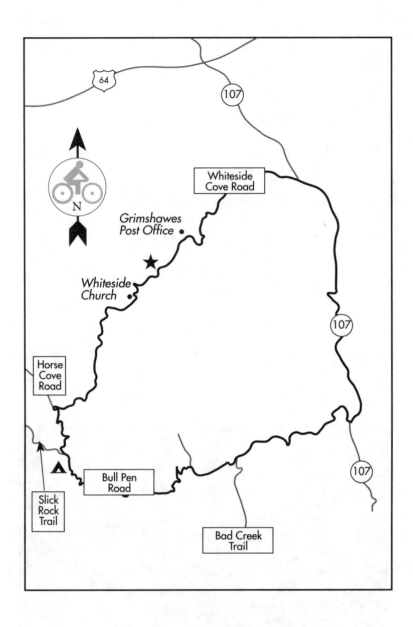

Whiteside Cove Road / Bull Pen Road Loop

Distance: 21.5 miles

Difficulty: Strenuous

Riding surface: Gravel road, dirt road, paved road

Maps: 1. USGS 7.5 minute quadrangle, Cashiers
2. USGS 7.5 minute quadrangle, Highlands
3. Nantahala National Forest Map

Access: From the junction of U.S. 64 and N.C. 107 in Cashiers, drive south on N.C. 107 for 1.8 miles to Whiteside Cove Road. Turn right and proceed 4.3 miles to a pull-off. Park here.

Elevation change: The ride begins at an elevation of 2,650 feet at the pull-off. It climbs to 3,000 feet at the intersection with Bull Pen Road. By the time Bull Pen Road passes the Slick Rock trailhead, the ride reaches 3,200 feet. The elevation drops to 2,600 feet at the iron bridge over the Chattooga River, then climbs to 3,200 feet at the intersection with N.C. 107. A maximum elevation of 3,400 feet is reached on this paved road. The elevation drops back to 2,650 feet on the descent to the parking pull-off. The total elevation gain is 1,350 feet.

Configuration: Loop

Whiteside Cove Road

This loop, offering both meandering dirt roads and popular attractions, will award serious cyclists with an outstanding, long mountain-bike ride.

It begins on Whiteside Cove Road, a scenic dirt road with a pleasant mix of moderate climbs and descents. From this road, cyclists are treated to views of Whiteside Mountain and the adjacent Devil's Courthouse. Whiteside Mountain's rugged stone face is a stark contrast to the rolling green mountains surrounding it. It is one of the most recognizable landmarks in the Highlands/Cashiers area and is the largest expanse of vertical sheer rock east of the Rocky Mountains.

After cycling past Whiteside Cove Church, which is on the left, you will continue for almost 2 miles to a spur trail leading to Granite City. This area, with its huge rocks and boulders, is a popular attraction.

Whiteside Cove Road intersects with Bull Pen Road at 3.5 miles. Slick Rock Trail is on the right after 1 mile on Bull Pen Road; this short, unmarked trail leads to a rock overlook which provides excellent views of the Chattooga River basin.

As you continue on Bull Pen Road, you will descend past

Ammons Branch Campground. Some sections of the road are washboard, so watch your speed. Ellicott Rock Trail is on the right about 0.5 mile past Ammons Branch. This trail leads down to the Chattooga River, where Ellicott Rock sits as a survey marker near the spot where Georgia, South Carolina, and North Carolina share a boundary. Just downstream is Commissioner Rock, the actual boundary of this tristate junction. Inscribed on this rock is "LAT 35 AD 1813 NC + SC."

After passing the Ellicott Rock trailhead, continue cycling about 1.5 miles to an old iron bridge which crosses the Chattooga River. This river, with its spectacular scenery, excellent water quality, and thrilling rapids, is one of the most popular whitewater rivers in the United States. In 1974, when it came under the protection of the National Wild and Scenic Rivers Act, it was made forever safe from development and dams. The Chattooga gained national notoriety when the movie Deliverance was filmed along sections of its banks. The river flows from North Carolina to form the natural border between Georgia and South Carolina for about 40 miles before emptying into Lake Tugaloo.

Bull Pen Road with its winding curves and good riding surface

The exceptionally beautiful scenery here will probably make you want to linger before continuing your mountain-bike ride.

The loop continues on Bull Pen Road for another 5.5 miles. You will make a left turn onto N.C. 107, which climbs for about 5 miles to Whiteside Cove Road. Before reaching your parked vehicle, you will pass Grimshawes post office, which will be on the right. This tiny shack is the nation's smallest post office, measuring only six feet by eight feet. The original building was constructed in 1875; the one standing today is a restored version.

0.0   From the pull-off, begin cycling Whiteside Cove Road.

0.7   Whiteside Cove Church is on the left.

2.4   The spur trail to Granite City is on the right.

3.5   You will arrive at an intersection with Horse Cove Road and Bull Pen Road. Turn left onto Bull Pen Road and begin climbing.

4.5   Slick Rock Trail is on the right.

4.8   Ammons Branch Campground is on the right.

5.3   Ellicott Rock Wilderness is on the right; continue straight.

6.6   You will cross the Chattooga River on an old iron bridge.

7.8   A gated road, F.R. 4564, is on the left. Continue straight. During winter's leaf-off season, a small waterfall is visible off to the right.

8.3   There is a fork in the road; bear to the right.

9.3   You will cross Fowler Creek. Continue straight.

Whiteside Mountain

Grimshawes post office, the smallest in the United States, on Whiteside Cove Road

9.4   Just after Fowler Creek, you will see the Bad Creek trailhead on the right. This trail leads to Ellicott Rock, Burrell's Ford on the Chattooga River, and the fish hatchery.

12.0   Bull Pen Road intersects with N.C. 107; turn left onto this highway and begin climbing.

17.2   Turn left onto Whiteside Cove Road.

20.2   Grimshawes post office is on the right.

21.5   You will arrive back at your vehicle.

Bull Pen Road

Chattooga River

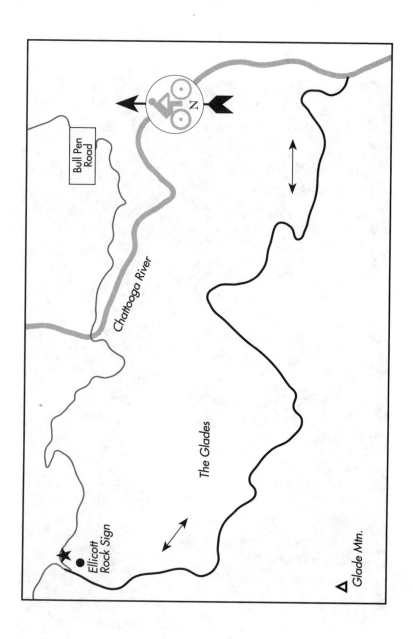

Glades Area Ride

Distance: 7.6 miles

Difficulty: Easy to moderate

Riding surface: Single-track trail

Maps: 1. USGS 7.5 minute quadrangle, Cashiers
2. USGS 7.5 minute quadrangle, Highlands
3. Nantahala National Forest Map

Access: From the junction of U.S. 64 and N.C. 107 in Cashiers, drive south on N.C. 107 for 7 miles. Turn right onto Bull Pen Road and drive 6.6 miles to the parking area next to the Ellicott Rock sign. Park here.

Elevation change: The ride begins at an elevation of 2,800 feet and climbs to 2,900 feet in the first few miles. It then drops to 2,300 feet at the banks of the Chattooga River. When retracing your path, you will climb another 600 feet before reaching the parking area. The total elevation gain is 700 feet.

Configuration: Out and back

T he Glades area south of Highlands features single-track trails that seem custom-made for mountain biking. The beautiful forest and the excellent views of the Chattooga River make this an extremely popular ride with local cyclists.

The ride begins on a level single-track trail that weaves through a mature hardwood forest accentuated with lacy hemlock, fern-filled ravines, and sun-dappled meadows. It maintains a level-to-descending grade on the approach to the river. Near the Chattooga, the trail threads through dense wetland flora such as rhododendron and mountain laurel.

The trail ends at the river near the tristate boundary of North Carolina, South Carolina, and Georgia. Ellicott Rock, located in the center of the Chattooga River, is a survey marker for the boundary. Just downstream is Commissioner Rock, the actual boundary of the three states. It is inscribed, "LAT 35 AD 1813 NC + SC." The namesakes of the two rocks—Messrs. Ellicott and Commissioner—were early surveyors.

0.0   The trail begins as a brief climb, then moderates to an easier grade.

0.4   At the intersection of trails, take the trail on the left.

The Chattooga River upstream of Commissioner Rock and Ellicott Rock

When the going gets too tough, you can always walk your bike

2.1   There is an intersection of trails on the edge of a meadow. Two trails bear left; take the trail closest to center.

2.7   You will come to another junction of trails; take the trail to the left. There are several whoop-de-dos in this section of the ride.

3.8   A narrow trail on the left leads down to the Chattooga River. Leave your bike here and hike about 0.5 mile to the water's edge. After returning to your bike, turn around and retrace your path.

7.6   You will arrive back at your vehicle.

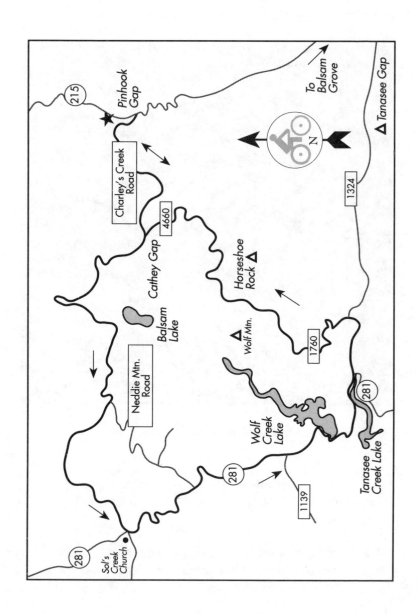

Wolf Mountain Loop

Distance: 26.8 miles

Difficulty: Strenuous

Riding surface: Dirt road, paved road

Maps: 1. USGS 7.5 minute quadrangle, Sam Knob
2. USGS 7.5 minute quadrangle, Tuckasegee
3. USGS 7.5 minute quadrangle, Big Ridge
4. USGS 7.5 minute quadrangle, Lake Toxaway
5. Nantahala National Forest Map

Access: From the junction of U.S. 178 and U.S. 64 near Rosman, drive west on U.S. 64 for 0.6 mile. Turn right onto N.C. 215 and proceed north for 12.8 miles to the intersection with Charley's Creek Road (F.R. 1756) at Pinhook Gap; there is a national-forest sign for Balsam Lake Recreation Area on the left. Turn left here and park at any pull-off.

Elevation change: The ride begins at an elevation of 4,200 feet at Pinhook Gap. You will descend to 3,800 feet at the bridge over Tanasee Creek, climb to 4,100 feet at Cathey Gap, then descend to 3,600 feet at the intersection with Neddie Mountain Road (S.R. 1757). A climb to 4,000 feet is countered by a descent to 3,500 feet at the intersection with N.C. 281. Next, you will descend to 3,000 feet at Wolf Lake before climbing along the ridge lines of Wolf Mountain to an elevation of 4,200 feet. You will drop to 4,000 feet and generally maintain this elevation until ascending briefly to 4,100 feet at Cathey Gap. You will then descend to 3,800 feet before making the final climb back up to 4,200 feet near Pinhook Gap. The total elevation gain is 2,400 feet.

Configuration: Loop

Christmas tree farms abound on the Wolf Mountain Loop

This loop of rustic dirt roads and sylvan countryside takes to the backroads of western North Carolina for a full day of mountain biking. The ride covers a wide range of territory, giving out-of-town cyclists a good, representative slice of the area.

The biggest attraction on this loop is the multitude of Christmas-tree farms that decorate the route. Each farm is divided into squares, with each square boasting trees at a particular stage of growth; the trees are thus grouped according to size. From a high overlook, these squares make the farms look like they have been blanketed with a calico quilt that has been snapped open and allowed to settle over the hills and valleys. Some sections of road wind right through these pastoral farms, bathing your nose with the pungent scent of evergreens. An early-November ride, before the holiday harvest, is a favorite time to cycle this loop.

The ride begins at Pinhook Gap and rolls across Wolf Mountain on Charley's Creek Road, passing through farmland and crossing a number of trickling streams. This dirt road runs into N.C. 281, a descending paved road which is a short connector on this ride. You will soon return to dirt road and then climb along the eastern slope of Wolf Mountain up to Horseshoe Rock. This is an arduous climb that will have you clicking into your granny gear in no time. Horseshoe Rock is a huge granite bald that looks like a horseshoe when viewed from above. You will then complete the ride by cycling to Cathey Gap and back to the starting point at Pinhook Gap.

0.0   Begin cycling Charley's Creek Road.

0.6   Pinhook Campground is on the left.

1.9   You will cross Tanasee Creek. A serious climb follows this crossing.

2.6   You will arrive at Cathey Gap. F.R. 4660 is on the left; continue straight.

Snow-covered forest service road

3.0 Charley's Creek Baptist Church is on the left.

4.9 You will cross Wolf Creek.

5.0 Harris Cemetery is on the right.

5.3 Balsam Lake is on the left.

5.9 Balsam Lodge is on the left.

7.6 The road intersects with Neddie Mountain Road. Continue straight.

10.6 The dirt road ends; continue straight to the stop sign.

10.7 The road intersects with N.C. 281. Dodgen Creek Church is on the right; straight ahead is F.R. 1138, which leads to Sol's Creek Church. Turn left onto N.C. 281 South.

12.5 F.R. 1179 is on the right; continue straight.

12.6 Neddie Mountain Road is on the left; continue descending on N.C. 281 South.

14.7 F.R. 1139 is on the right; continue straight.

15.4 You will approach a dam on Wolf Lake. On the left are two forest-service roads that lead down to the lake. Cycle over the dam, which leads back to a dirt road.

16.7 Tanasee Creek Reservoir is on the right.

17.0 There is a fork in the road; bear left on F.R. 1762.

18.0 There is an intersection of forest-service roads; bear left on F.R. 1760 and begin another climb.

20.9   Horseshoe Rock is on the right. This makes a good resting spot after the last few miles of serious climbing on loose gravel.

21.4   The trail narrows and enters a pine forest.

24.2   There is a T-intersection; turn right onto Charley's Creek Road.

24.9   You will cross Tanasee Creek.

26.3   Pinhook Campground is on the right. You will descend briefly, then continue with a climb.

26.8   You will arrive back at your parked vehicle at the intersection with N.C. 215.

Christmas tree farm on Wolf Mountain Loop

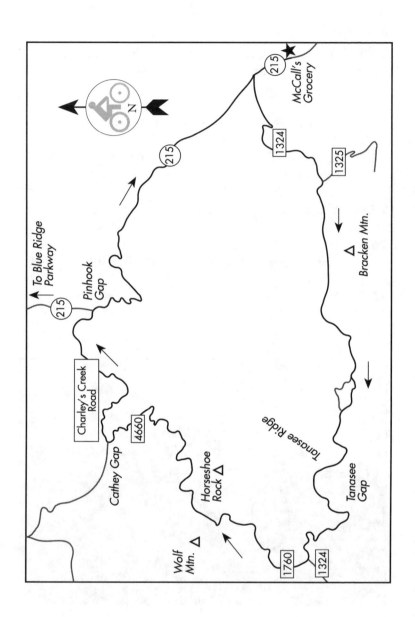

Tanasee Ridge Loop

Distance: 22.3 miles

Difficulty: Strenuous

Riding surface: Dirt road, paved road

Maps: 1. USGS 7.5 minute quadrangle, Rosman
2. USGS 7.5 minute quadrangle, Lake Toxaway
3. USGS 7.5 minute quadrangle, Sam Knob
4. Nantahala National Forest Map

Access: From the junction of U.S. 178 and U.S. 64, drive west on U.S. 64 for 0.6 mile. Turn right onto N.C. 215 and proceed north for 7.3 miles to McCall's Grocery Store. Stop in, buy a snack if you wish, and ask permission to park. You can also park across the street.

Elevation change: The ride begins at an elevation of 2,850 feet on N.C. 215 at the junction with F.R. 1324. It climbs to 3,500 feet at Tanasee Gap and then descends to 3,200 feet at the junction of F.R. 1324 and F.R. 1760. The ride climbs to a maximum of 4,200 feet at Horseshoe Rock before descending back to 2,850 feet at the junction with N.C. 215. The total elevation gain is 1,650 feet.

Configuration: Loop

T his long mountain-bike ride winds through idyllic countryside while climbing tough hills and descending through verdant valleys. There is a myriad of Christmas tree farms along the way, which adds special interest to the ride. You will climb a rambling dirt road up mountain slopes to high-elevation overlooks. These vistas give cyclists a bird's-eye view of hillsides studded with hundreds of dark green Fraser firs. At lower elevations, the road cleaves a path between farms, giving mountain bikers an up-close perspective. The gentle waft of breezes will deliver the fresh scent of evergreens as you cycle by.

The ride begins near McCall's Grocery Store in Balsam Grove, a small mountain hamlet where more than half the residents are named McCall. You might want to stop at the store for a Moon Pie, an RC Cola, and a chance to pet the old hound dog sleeping out front.

The ride continues with a turn onto a pastoral dirt road which climbs over Tanasee Ridge and through Tanasee Gap. It joins a different dirt road before climbing to Horseshoe Rock, a sheer-rock boulder which gets its name from its appearance from the air. A right turn at Cathey Gap leads to Pinhook Gap and the intersection with N.C. 215. A swift descent on this paved road will lead you back to the starting point.

0.0   From McCall's Grocery Store, turn right onto N.C. 215 and cycle north.

0.5   Turn left onto F.R. 1324, which begins as a paved road but soon changes to dirt. The road parallels Jake Branch for a short distance.

2.0   You will reach a junction with F.R. 1325; bear right to continue on F.R. 1324, which parallels Tucker Creek.

2.3   You will cross Tucker Creek.

3.1   You will cross Bracken Creek. The road continues along the northern base of Bracken Mountain.

Dirt road on the Tanasee Ridge Loop

5.0 There is a gated road on the left; continue straight.

5.6 Woods Church Road is on the right; continue straight.

6.8 You will cycle through Tanasee Gap and across Cold Creek.

8.0 You will reach an intersection with F.R. 1760; turn right.

10.9 Horseshoe Rock is on the right.

14.2 You will arrive at an intersection at Cathey Gap. Turn right onto Charley's Creek Road (F.R. 1756).

14.9 You will cross Tanasee Creek and begin a climb.

16.3 Pinhook Campground is on the right.

21.8 F.R. 1324 is on the right; continue straight for another 0.5 mile to McCall's Grocery Store.

22.3 You will arrive back at your vehicle.

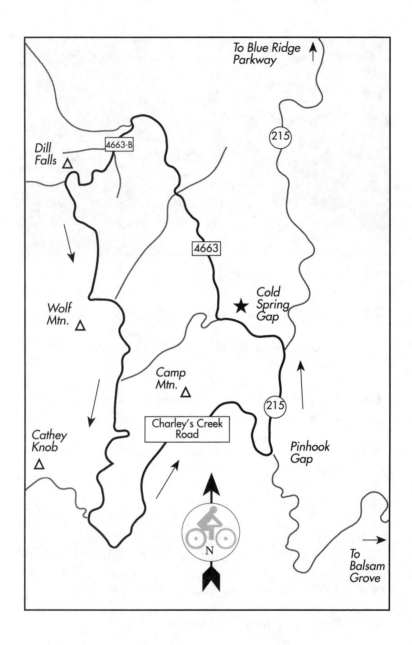

Dill Falls /
Pinhook Valley Loop

Distance: 7.4 miles

Difficulty: Easy to moderate

Riding surface: Dirt road, single-track trail, brief section of paved road

Map: USGS 7.5 minute quadrangle, Sam Knob

Access: From the intersection of U.S. 64 and N.C. 215, drive 12.3 miles on N.C. 215 North. Turn left onto F.R. 4663, a dirt road which runs through a small community of homes. After driving 0.4 mile, park at any of the pull-offs.

Elevation change: The ride begins at an elevation of 4,300 feet on F.R. 4663. It descends to 4,200 feet at Dill Falls and to a minimum of 3,800 feet at the intersection with Charley's Creek Road (F.R. 1756) in Pinhook Valley. You will then begin a climb which reaches 4,200 feet at the intersection with N.C. 215 at Pinhook Gap and 4,300 feet back on F.R. 4663. The total elevation gain is 500 feet.

Configuration: Loop

Crossing Tanasee Creek

This is an excellent mountain-bike ride for cyclists of diverse abilities. Highlights such as premium single-track trails, scenic dirt roads, fun creek crossings, meadows, and a beautiful waterfall promise a fine day of cycling.

The ride begins on a rambling dirt road which follows an easy grade along the western slope of Tanasee Ridge. It then turns onto a heavily canopied single-track trail which leads to the base of Dill Falls. This exceptional waterfall spills several hundred feet over a cliff into Tanasee Creek. You will then plunge through the icy waters of Tanasee Creek to continue.

The single-track follows Tanasee Creek for most of its length before spilling into a T-intersection with Charley's Creek Road in Pinhook Valley. A left turn on this dirt road will lead you on a long, steady ascent to Pinhook Gap. You will meander past several picturesque Christmas-tree farms, which will help take your mind off the climb. At Pinhook Gap, you will cycle a brief section of paved road which leads to F.R. 4663 and the end of the ride.

0.0   From the pull-off, begin cycling down F.R. 4663.

1.4   A trail crosses the road; continue straight.

1.5   There is a fork in the road; bear left on F.R. 4663B.

2.0   You will reach an intersection. A new logging road continues straight, an old logging road heads right, and an old jeep road bears right between the two logging roads. Follow the middle road, the old jeep road.

2.2   Dill Falls is on the right. Cross Tanasee Creek to continue.

2.3   You will come to a junction of trails; make a hard left turn to continue.

2.8   The trail enters a meadow.

2.9   You will cycle through a creek.

Christmas tree farm

Dill Falls

3.0 You will reach an intersection of trails; continue straight.

3.2 You will come to another intersection of trails; turn right.

3.6 You will cross a small creek; bear right to continue.

4.5 The trail ends at Charley's Creek Road; turn left.

6.5 You will come to an intersection with N.C. 215; turn left.

7.0 Turn left onto F.R. 4663.

7.4 You will arrive back at your vehicle at the pull-off on F.R. 4663.

Horsepasture Area

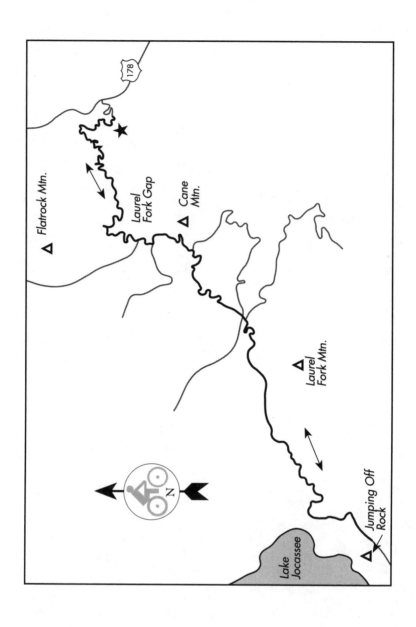

Rocky Bottom /
Jumping Off Rock Ride

Distance: 19.2 miles

Difficulty: Moderate to strenuous

Riding surface: Dirt road

Maps: 1. USGS 7.5 minute quadrangle, Eastatoe Gap
2. USGS 7.5 minute quadrangle, Reid

Access: From the intersection of S.C. 11 and U.S. 178, proceed north on U.S. 178 for 8 miles. Turn left. You will immediately come to a fork. Take the right fork and proceed 0.3 mile to a large gravel parking area on the left. Park here.

Elevation change: The ride begins at an elevation of 1,650 feet at the parking lot. It climbs to 2,400 feet at Cane Mountain and maintains this elevation for several miles before descending to about 2,000 feet at the Jumping Off Rock overlook. When you retrace your path, you will climb back to 2,400 feet at Cane Mountain and then descend to the parking lot. The total elevation gain is about 1,150 feet.

Configuration: Out and back

View of Lake Jocassee on the ride to Jumping Off Rock

T his ride begins on a scenic dirt road which gently winds through a forest of mixed hardwoods and conifers. After about 4 miles, it climbs Cane Mountain and continues along the southern slope of Laurel Fork Mountain. There are several overlooks along the way featuring panoramic views of the surrounding mountains and the Laurel Fork Creek basin.

When you reach the overlook at Jumping Off Rock, you will probably want to linger to enjoy the outstanding views. According to legend, this was the site where two young Indians, forbidden by their tribe to marry, joined hands and leapt to their death. The site is known by some as "Lover's Leap."

Lake Jocassee's name also comes from the Cherokee heritage. Jocassee was an Indian princess whose lover, Toxaway, was killed by her brother, Chief Oconee. In her grief, Jocassee went out on the river in her canoe and saw the spirit of Toxaway beneath the water. Princess Jocassee leapt from the boat to join him and was never seen again. Many of the names of creeks and rivers in this area come from Indian lore.

0.0 From the parking lot, turn left onto the dirt road to begin the ride.

0.2 Eastatoe Creek Heritage Preserve is on the left.

3.4 You will reach an intersection of forest-service roads; bear left.

3.5 You will reach another intersection of forest-service roads; bear left again.

4.2 As you arrive at the top of the ridge, the grade levels out and the condition of the road improves.

7.7 There is an excellent view from an overlook on the right.

8.6 A gated road is on the right; continue straight.

8.7 There is a camping area on the right.

Sheer rock cliffs along Lake Jocassee

Narrow, hard-packed dirt road in the Horsepasture area

8.9   You will reach a fork in the road. There is a grass road to the left; bear right on the high road.

9.0   A utility tower is on the right; the road passes under power lines.

9.6   You will reach Jumping Off Rock, which is on the right side of the road. There is a pull-off on the right. Exercise caution in this area—stay away from the edge. This rock has a precipitous drop-off, and the ground is covered with pine needles that are very slippery when wet. The road to Jumping Off Rock continues toward Jocassee Dam, but this ride turns around at this point. To return to the starting point, retrace your path.

19.2   You will arrive back at the parking area.

View of Lake Jocassee from Jumping Off Rock

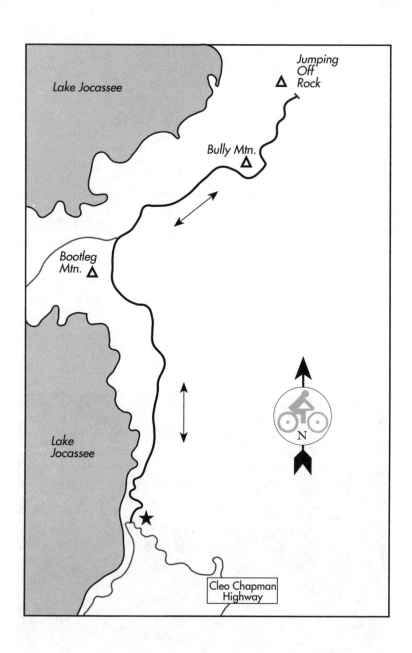

Lake Jocassee

Jumping
Off
Rock

Bully Mtn.

Bootleg
Mtn.

Lake
Jocassee

N

Cleo Chapman
Highway

Lake Jocassee /
Jumping Off Rock Ride

Distance: 7.6 miles

Difficulty: Moderate

Riding surface: Dirt road

Maps: 1. USGS 7.5 minute quadrangle, Reid
2. USGS 7.5 minute quadrangle, Salem

Access: From the intersection of U.S. 178 and S.C. 11, proceed west on S.C. 11 for 10.4 miles. Turn right onto Roy F. Jones Road. You will cross Eastatoe Creek after 1.3 miles. At 2.2 miles, you will reach a junction of roads; bear left. At 2.4 miles, bear left onto Cleo Chapman Highway at the intersection. Continue driving until the paved road ends after 5.6 miles. Park at any of the pull-offs near the beginning of the dirt road.

Elevation change: The ride starts at an elevation of 1,000 feet at the beginning of the dirt road. It climbs to 1,600 feet, then drops briefly to 1,500 feet at the fork in the road. It begins climbing again, reaching a maximum elevation of 2,000 feet at the Jumping Off Rock overlook. The total elevation gain is 1,100 feet.

Configuration: Out and back

Sunset on Lake Jocassee

This ride is a much shorter version of its counterpart in the previous chapter. It begins on a scenic dirt road which steadily climbs through a mature forest. The ride is spiced with occasional views of Lake Jocassee.

There is a fork in the road at the 2-mile mark. Turn right to cycle to Jumping Off Rock, a granite rockface overlooking the lake. This is the legendary site from which two young Indians, forbidden by their tribe to marry, joined hands and leapt to their death.

0.0   From the parking pull-off, cycle down the dirt road.

2.0   There is a fork in the road; bear right. (A left turn leads to a point on Lake Jocassee surrounded by azure waters; if you choose to cycle this dirt road, you will add 3.6 miles to the ride.)

3.8   You will reach Jumping Off Rock. To continue the ride, turn around and retrace your path.

7.6   You will arrive back at your parked vehicle at the end of the dirt road.

Steep, technical dirt road leading to Lake Jocassee

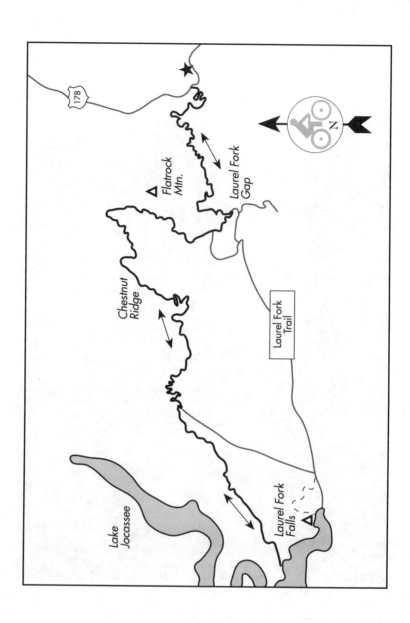

Rocky Bottom /
Lake Jocassee Peninsula Ride

Distance: 22 miles

Difficulty: Strenuous

Riding surface: Dirt road, single-track trail

Maps: 1. USGS 7.5 minute quadrangle, Eastatoe Gap
2. USGS 7.5 minute quadrangle, Reid

Access: From the intersection of S.C. 11 and U.S. 178, proceed north on U.S. 178 for 8 miles. Turn left. You will immediately come to a fork. Take the right fork and drive 0.3 mile to the large gravel parking area on the left.

Elevation change: The ride begins at an elevation of 1,650 feet at the parking area. It climbs to 2,000 feet at the junction at 3.5 miles and to a maximum of 2,800 feet at the ridge summit. It drops to 1,900 feet at the junction with the road leading to the Lake Jocassee peninsula, then to a minimum of 1,200 feet near the lake. As you retrace your path, you will climb to 1,900 feet at the intersection and 2,800 feet at the top of the ridge before descending back to the parking lot. The total elevation gain is a whopping 2,750 feet. Have you had your Wheaties today?

Configuration: Out and back

This is a heart-pounding, leg-burning, grueling ride for hard-core cyclists only. If you are looking for a challenge or are simply a masochist, then this is the ride for you.

This is the only mountain-bike ride I have ever cycled where I semiseriously thought that I might not make it back. Had there been a decent spot to land a rescue helicopter to airlift me out, I probably would have thrown my bike over the ridge and into the lake. Then again, I have strong moral convictions against littering. Besides, I don't think I had enough strength left to hoist my bike over my shoulders to throw it.

The ride begins on a pleasant dirt road that is bordered by a mixed-hardwood forest. The sound of trickling streams nearby will lull you into thinking you are going to have a nice day cycling in the woods. Ha! You will soon find yourself climbing a technical, bony dirt road.

After about 8 miles, you will turn onto a descending, sandy jeep road. This road parallels the Foothills Trail for a brief distance as it descends toward Lake Jocassee. You might want to enjoy the views at the lake and refuel on your power bars before retracing your path and climbing out. This is an excruciating climb that will humble even expert cyclists into dismounting. By

Dirt road through the Horsepasture area

the time you finish the ride, there will be no question as to whether you have had a good aerobic workout.

0.0 From the parking area, turn left onto the dirt road.

0.2 Eastatoe Creek Heritage Preserve is on the left.

3.4 You will reach an intersection of forest-service roads; take the right fork. Cycle around the gate to begin a serious, moderately technical climb.

5.5 You will reach the top of the ridge.

5.6 There is a gated forest-service road on the right; continue straight for a fast, thrilling descent.

Steep climb from Lake Jocassee

Eastatoe Creek

6.3   A gated road is on the right; continue straight.

8.4   You will come to a fork in the road; take the right fork onto a sandy jeep road to descend to Lake Jocassee.

9.4   Foothills Trail crosses the road.

9.5 A gated road is on the left; continue straight.

10.5 You will cycle under a utility tower; turn left at the junction of trails.

11.0 The trail ends near the lake. Enjoy this scenic resting spot before turning around and retracing your path.

22.0 You will arrive back at the parking area.

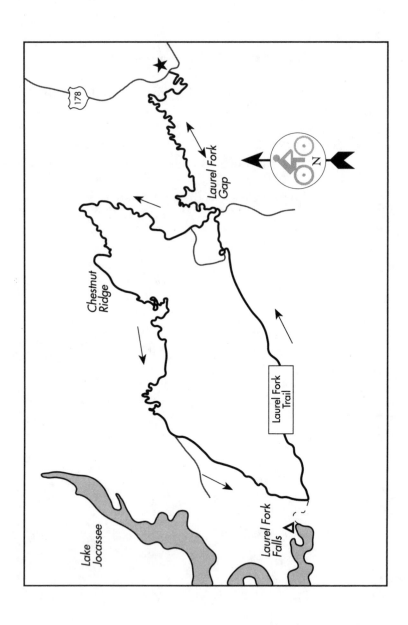

Rocky Bottom / Laurel Fork Creek Loop

Distance: 17.1 miles

Difficulty: Moderate to strenuous

Riding surface: Dirt road

Maps: 1. USGS 7.5 minute quadrangle, Eastatoe Gap
2. USGS 7.5 minute quadrangle, Reid

Access: From the intersection of U.S. 178 and S.C. 11, take U.S. 178 east toward Rosman. Drive 8 miles, then turn left onto a dirt road. Bear right almost immediately onto another dirt road. (Bearing left will take you down to Laurel Valley Lodge and Restaurant.) Drive 0.3 mile to the large gravel parking area on the left. You will see a sign for the Foothills Trail.

Elevation change: The ride begins at an elevation of 1,650 feet at the parking area. It climbs to 2,000 feet at the right turn at 3.5 miles and to a maximum of 2,800 feet at the ridge summit. The ride drops to 1,200 feet at Laurel Fork Creek, then climbs for several miles until it reaches 2,000 feet again. On the way back to the parking lot, the elevation drops to 1,650 feet. The total elevation gain is 1,950 feet.

Configuration: Loop

Laurel Fork Creek

This mountain-bike ride winds through the Horsepasture area of upstate South Carolina. According to local legend, this region was used by Confederates to hide horses from Union soldiers during the Civil War. That was long before Lake Jocassee came into existence, so there were plenty of low-lying areas to utilize.

The loop begins on a dirt road that weaves through a deciduous forest with an occasional evergreen stand. During the first few miles, you will cycle past several cold mountain springs trickling over glistening black rock. During the spring, the forest is filled with blooming dogwoods, Fraser magnolias, violets, and a verdant glen of Christmas ferns.

A serious technical climb begins at 3.5 miles. There is little tree canopy to shade this section of road, so during the summer months, it is typically hot, dry, and dusty. After this climb comes a thrilling descent which will lead you to the low-lying area of Laurel Fork Creek.

You will make several creek crossings, the first of which is over a suspension bridge. The remaining crossings are either over wooden footbridges or via fords through the water. The creek crossings are cool and quite refreshing during the summer but icily cold in the winter. You will have to cycle the last few miles with wet feet, so avoid this ride during cold weather.

Giant virgin hemlocks can be seen along the banks of Laurel Fork Creek. In late March and early April, look for Oconee bells (Shortia galacifolia), a rare and endangered wildflower indigenous to the southern Appalachians of South Carolina and Georgia. This wildflower is of special interest to botanists, as it was not found again for nearly a century after its initial discovery. The white, bell-shaped blossoms hang from erect, leafless stalks. The leaves are long, rounded evergreen with scalloped margins. The plant resembles galax, but its leaves are smaller and its flowers are solitary. If you are fortunate enough to spot a stand of Oconee bells, observe them, photograph them, but do not disturb them.

You will climb away from the creek toward the end of the ride. The last few miles back to the parking area are on a level-to-descending grade. It is the perfect end to an excellent mountain-bike ride.

0.0   From the parking lot, turn left onto the dirt road to begin the ride.

0.2   Eastatoe Creek Heritage Preserve is on the left.

Dark green rhododendron leaves contrast against gray granite walls

3.4 You will come to a fork in the road; take the right fork.

3.7 The Foothills Trail crosses the dirt road you are cycling.

5.6 You will reach a fork in the road; continue straight. You will be descending at this point.

6.3 There is a gated road on the right; continue straight.

8.4 You will arrive at a fork in the road; bear left.

8.5 You will come to a gate across the road; cycle around it to continue.

10.4 There is another gate across the road; again, cycle around it.

10.5 Just past the gate, you will reach a T-intersection. Turn left and cross Laurel Fork Creek on the suspension bridge. (Note: If you want to view Laurel Fork Falls, turn right at this intersection. This optional spur trail will add about 1 mile to the ride.)

13.5 There is a gate across the road; continue straight.

13.6 You will arrive at an intersection of dirt roads; bear left.

13.7 You will see a road that makes a sharp left turn; bear right at the fork.

17.1 You will arrive back at the parking area.

Horsepasture area

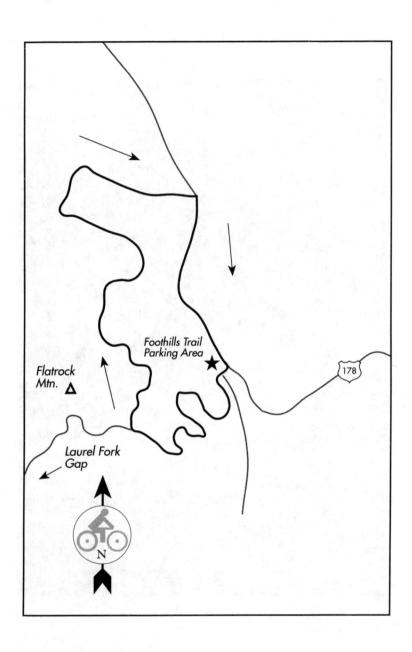

Flatrock
Mtn. △

Foothills Trail
Parking Area
★

178

Laurel Fork
Gap

N

Horsepasture Lagniappe

Distance: 2 miles

Difficulty: Easy to moderate

Riding surface: Single-track trail, dirt road, paved road

Map: USGS 7.5 minute quadrangle, Eastatoe Gap

Access: From the intersection of S.C. 11 and U.S. 178, proceed north on U.S. 178 for 8 miles. Turn left. You will immediately come to a fork. Take the right fork and proceed 0.3 mile to a large gravel parking area on the left.

Elevation change: The ride begins at 1,650 feet and climbs quickly to a maximum elevation of 1,900 feet. The total elevation gain is 250 feet.

Configuration: Loop

Mechanical breakdown in the boonies

Mountain biking in the Horsepasture area

Lagniappe is a popular term in southern Louisiana which means "a little something extra." This short ride is just that. It can be ridden after one of the other Horsepasture rides described in the preceding chapters, or it can be ridden when time is short and daylight is running out.

The ride begins on a rambling dirt road which winds through a heavily wooded area. It continues as a climbing single-track trail accented with berms. The grade levels out, then begins a serious, short climb that will test your technical skills—if you can maintain enough forward momentum to stay on your bike. This climb is followed by a gentle descent through a forest of white pines that will lead you back to U.S. 178. A right turn on this paved highway will return you to the starting point.

0.0 From the parking area, turn left onto the dirt road.

0.7 Turn right onto a wide dirt trail. You will climb briefly over several berms before bearing left.

0.9 You will reach a fork in the trail. Continue straight up the steep clay hill; you will probably have to push your bike here. (The trail to the left leads back to the main road.)

1.0 There is another fork in the trail; continue straight.

1.2 The trail ends at U.S. 178; turn right and descend on this paved road.

1.7 Turn right onto the dirt road, which leads back to the parking area.

2.0 You will arrive back at the parking area.

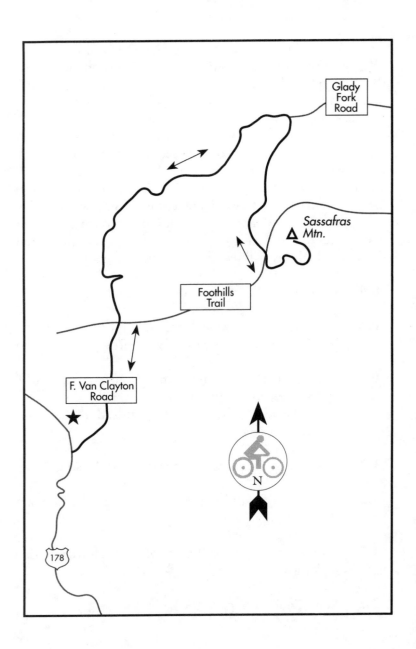

Sassafras Mountain Ride

Distance: 10 miles

Difficulty: Moderate to strenuous

Riding surface: Paved road

Map: USGS 7.5 minute quadrangle, Eastatoe Gap

Access: From the intersection of S.C. 11 and U.S. 178, proceed north on U.S. 178 for 7.1 miles. Turn right onto F. Van Clayton Road; there is a sign for the Rocky Bottom Camp of the Blind. Park at any of the pull-offs on this road.

Elevation change: The ride begins at an elevation of 1,750 feet at Rocky Bottom. It steadily climbs, reaching 2,400 feet at Chimney Top Gap, 2,800 feet at Folly Gap, and 3,554 feet at Sassafras Mountain. The total elevation gain is about 1,800 feet.

Configuration: Out and back

Nearing the summit of Sassafras Mountain

This ride leads through beautiful forest as it steadily climbs to the highest point in South Carolina—3,554 feet at Sassafras Mountain. It never leaves paved road and is a good option during wet weather, when single-track trails should be avoided by mountain bikers. The climb is grueling at times, but the thrilling descent makes the work worthwhile.

An old fire tower once sat atop Sassafras Mountain and could be climbed for outstanding 360-degree views of Greenville, South Carolina, and Mount Pisgah, on the Blue Ridge Parkway in North Carolina. The tower has been removed, but the great views remain.

The Foothills Trail passes over Sassafras Mountain and offers several interesting historical highlights. A short hike along this trail will take you by the remains of the homesite of John L. Cantrell, one of South Carolina's earliest settlers. If you continue east for another 2 miles, you will find yourself walking along the old roadbed of the Emory Gap Toll Road. This was the only road crossing the mountains from Pickens in the early 1900s; folks would lead ox-drawn covered wagons through these steep areas after paying a toll of $1.25. Two more miles of hiking will take you past Drawbar Cliffs, below which is located "the Lighthouse," a cave used by coon hunters for overnight protection from the elements.

0.0   Begin the ride by climbing F. Van Clayton Road, a paved road.

1.4   The Foothills Trail crosses the road; continue straight. You will begin a descent.

3.3   Glady Fork Road is on the left; bear right to continue.

4.3   A wooden sign on your right indicates the direction and mileage to Chimney Top Gap and Sassafras Mountain.

4.7   There is a large gravel parking area on the left. Continue straight up the climbing road and cycle around the gate to reach the top of Sassafras Mountain.

5.0   You will arrive at the top of Sassafras Mountain. Turn around and retrace your path.

10.0   You will arrive back at your parked vehicle at the intersection with U.S. 178.

View of nearby mountains from the peak of Sassafras Mountain

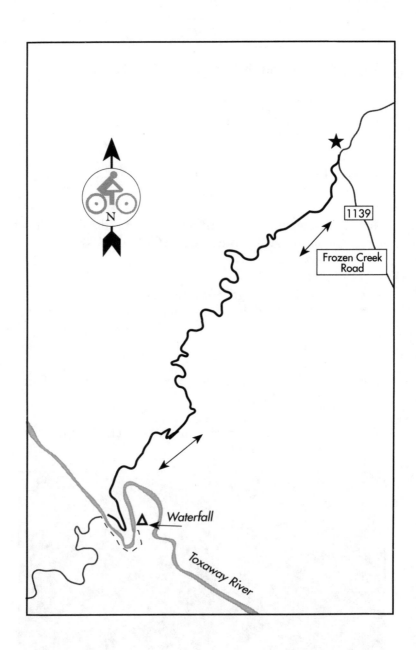

Toxaway River Ride

Distance: 7 miles

Difficulty: Moderate

Riding surface: Dirt road

Map: USGS 7.5 minute quadrangle, Reid

Access: From the junction of U.S. 178 and U.S. 64 in Rosman, proceed 2.5 miles on U.S. 64 West. Turn left onto Frozen Creek Road. Drive 0.8 mile to a fork; bear left and continue an additional 2.1 miles. The trail begins on the right. Park at any of the pull-offs near the trailhead.

Elevation change: The ride begins at an elevation of 2,200 feet at Frozen Creek Road and drops to 1,600 feet at the Toxaway River. You will then climb back to the starting elevation of 2,200 feet at Frozen Creek Road. The total elevation gain is 600 feet.

Configuration: Out and back

Crossing Toxaway River

This mountain-bike ride winds through exceptionally beautiful surroundings. The dirt road is heavily canopied with the limbs of mature hardwoods, lacy hemlocks, and pines. The forest is filled with rhododendron and dogwoods, whose white and pink blossoms make the scenery especially enjoyable during the spring.

If you would like to take an optional hiking trip, you can ford the Toxaway River for a walk to a secluded waterfall about 1 mile downstream. The area is thick with doghobble, an understory plant appropriately named for its "grabby" vines. If you elect not to take the strenuous hike to the waterfall, you can keep your feet dry by turning around before the river and retracing your path to the starting point.

0.0   The ride begins on a trail which crosses a small creek on a rickety wooden footbridge. You will then squeeze through a jumble of large boulders and cycle around a steel gate.

0.2   You will reach a fork in the road; take the right fork and begin a moderate climb.

0.6   There is another fork in the road; take the right fork and descend on a steep clay road.

1.8   You will reach a fork in the road; bear left.

3.1   There is a gated logging road on the right; continue straight.

3.5   You will reach the Toxaway River. (If you want to take the optional hike to the waterfall, ford the river at this point. Note: This is a river, not a small stream. At high-water levels, the river is deep and the currents are dangerously swift. Do not attempt to ford the river when conditions are unfavorable. After crossing, turn left at the fork and cycle 0.1 mile to the end of the road. There are a number of campsites in this area. Leave your bike here and hike downstream along the bank for about 1 mile. Since there is no established trail to follow, this is a strenuous outdoor experience. You will be able to hear the waterfall on your approach. After viewing the falls, retrace your path to your bicycle. Cross the Toxaway River to where you began this optional trip.) To return to the starting point, retrace your path on the dirt road back to Frozen Creek Road.

7.0   You will arrive back at your vehicle.

Forest-lined, dirt road leading to Toxaway River

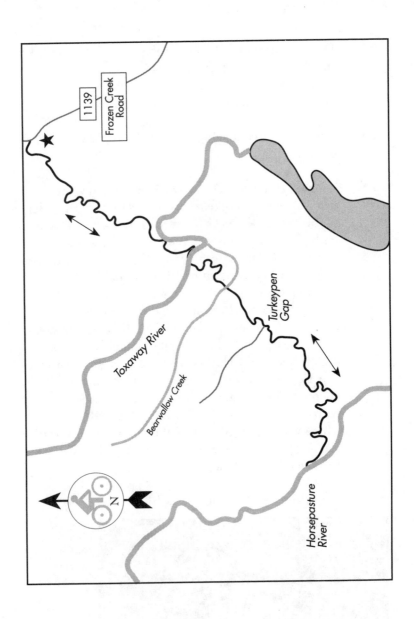

Two River Ride

Distance: 18 miles

Difficulty: Strenuous

Riding surface: Dirt road

Map: USGS 7.5 minute quadrangle, Reid

Access: From the junction of U.S. 178 and U.S. 64 in Rosman, proceed on U.S. 64 West for 2.5 miles. Turn left onto Frozen Creek Road. Drive 0.8 mile to a fork; bear left and continue an additional 2.1 miles. There is a trail on the right. Park at any of the pull-offs near the trailhead.

Elevation change: The ride begins at an elevation of 2,200 feet at Frozen Creek Road and drops to 1,600 feet at the Toxaway River crossing. Next, the road climbs to 1,700 feet and drops to 1,600 feet at the Bearwallow Creek crossing. It then climbs to 1,800 feet at Turkey Pen Gap before dropping to a minimum of 1,200 feet at the Horsepasture River. You will then turn around and retrace your path, climbing to 1,800 feet, dropping to 1,600 feet at Bearwallow Creek, climbing to 1,700 feet, and then dropping to 1,600 feet at the Toxaway River before making the final climb back to 2,200 feet at Frozen Creek Road. The total elevation gain is 1,600 feet.

Configuration: Out and back

Waterfall on Bearwallow Creek

This strenuous ride climbs and descends through a beautiful, mature forest. The long, gradual climbs are not terribly steep, but their length may have you pedaling in your lowest gear. You will also have to ford the Toxaway River—a frigid experience even in the summer. The river snakes through the mountains before emptying into Lake Jocassee several miles downstream.

The ride continues with a climb and then a long, fast descent across Bearwallow Creek and on to the Horsepasture River. Once at the river, you will turn around and begin retracing your path.

There are a number of excellent, secluded campsites along both rivers. If you are interested in draping your bike with filled panniers for a bikepacking excursion, this area of the Horsepasture is ideal for an overnight trip or even a full weekend. There are also a number of gated roads and single-track trails branching off the main dirt road which offer good exploratory rides.

0.0   The ride begins on a trail which crosses a small creek on a rickety wooden footbridge. You will then squeeze through a jumble of large boulders and cycle around a steel gate.

0.2   You will reach a fork in the road; take the right fork and begin a moderate climb.

0.6   There is another fork in the road; take the right fork and descend on a steep clay road.

1.8   You will come to a fork in the road; bear left.

3.1   There is a gated logging road on the right; continue straight.

3.5   You will reach the Toxaway River. You may want to take off your shoes and socks before fording. (Note: This is a river, not a small stream, and should be regarded as such. At high-water levels, the river is deep and the currents are dangerously swift. Do not attempt to ford the river when conditions are unfavorable.)

4.5   You will reach Bearwallow Creek. Continue across the creek.

5.5   There is a trail on the right at Turkeypen Gap; continue straight.

6.8   There is a fork in the road; bear left.

9.0   You will reach the Horsepasture River. Turn around and begin retracing your path.

18.0   You will reach Frozen Creek Road and the end of the ride.

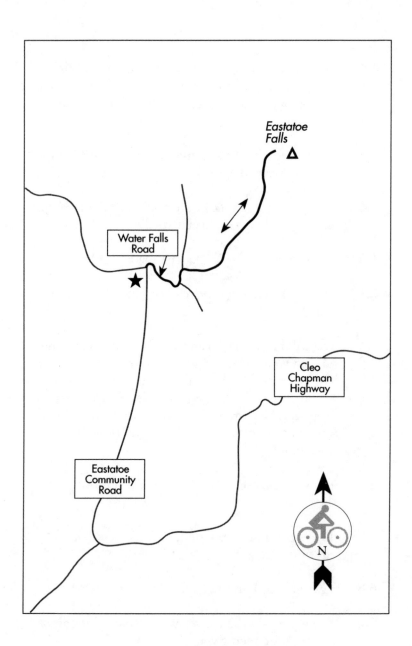

Eastatoe Falls

Water Falls Road

Cleo Chapman Highway

Eastatoe Community Road

N

Eastatoe Falls Ride

Distance: 1.8 miles

Difficulty: Easy

Riding surface: Dirt road, single-track trail

Map: USGS 7.5 minute quadrangle, Eastatoe Gap

Access: From the junction of U.S. 178 and S.C. 11, proceed on U.S. 178 North for 3.2 miles to Cleo Chapman Highway, named in honor of the woman who delivered mail to the people of this area for nearly half a century, during which time rain, sleet, or snow deterred her in her rounds only once. Turn left on Cleo Chapman Highway and proceed 2 miles to Eastatoe Community Road. Turn right and drive 0.9 mile to Water Falls Road. Park at any of the pull-offs.

Elevation change: The ride begins at an elevation of 1,000 feet and gradually climbs to a maximum of 1,150 feet. You will then turn around and descend back to 1,000 feet at the road. The total elevation gain is 150 feet.

Configuration: Out and back

Cycling the Eastatoe Falls Trail

T his ride could easily be called "Mountain Biking 101." An excellent introduction to the sport, it winds through a beautiful forest of hardwoods and pines on a mostly level grade. There are a number of highlights, including a stop at the foot of Eastatoe Falls, known by locals as Twin Falls. These two waterfalls drop several hundred feet in a thundering, awesome series of cascades.

This is an ideal ride for children and beginners.

0.0　From the pull-off, begin cycling on Water Falls Road. You will pass several homesteads.

0.3　Turn right at the junction of roads.

0.5　The road ends at a sign marking the nature preserve for Eastatoe Falls. Cycle through the gravel parking area and around the steel gate to continue.

0.7 A side trail on the right leads down to a creek. After exploring this trail, continue straight. The trail narrows and begins a gentle climb toward the falls. The prolific ground cover flanking the trail is called partridge berry.

0.9 The trail ends at the foot of Eastatoe Falls. Turn around and begin retracing your path.

1.8 You will reach the end of Water Falls Road and arrive back at your vehicle.

Eastatoe Falls

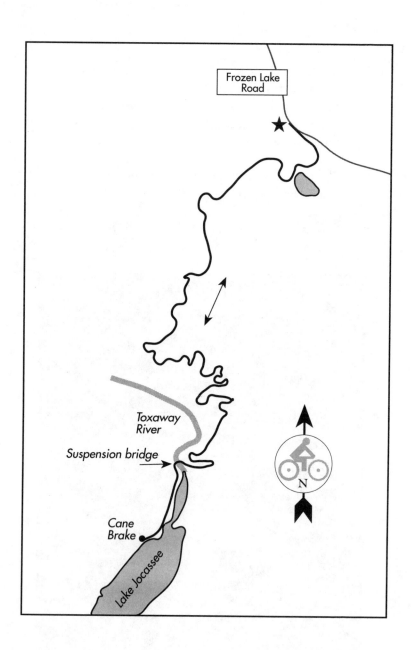

Cane Brake Ride

Distance: 10.2 miles

Difficulty: Moderate

Riding surface: Dirt road

Map: USGS 7.5 minute quadrangle, Reid

Access: From the junction of U.S. 178 and U.S. 64 in Rosman, proceed 2.5 miles on U.S. 64 West. Turn left onto Frozen Creek Road. Drive 0.8 mile to a fork; bear left to continue. Drive an additional 3.4 miles to a dirt road which begins on the right. Park at any pull-off near the dirt road.

Elevation change: The ride begins at 2,000 feet on Frozen Creek Road. The elevation remains the same for the first few miles and then drops to a minimum of 1,200 feet at Lake Jocassee. On the return trip, the ride climbs back to 2,000 feet at Frozen Creek Road. The total elevation gain is 800 feet.

Configuration: Out and back

Lake Jocassee

This ride descends along a scenic dirt road past Frozen Lake, a small, popular fishing area. It winds through a beautiful forest of mature hardwoods, delicate hemlocks, and mountain laurel. You will cross several creeks before reaching the end of the ride.

The Foothills Trail, which runs from Table Rock State Park to the Georgia border on the Chattooga River, joins the dirt road at the Toxaway River. You will cross the river on a sturdy suspension bridge built by the Duke Power Company.

A short ride along the northern finger of Lake Jocassee will bring you to an area known as Cane Brake. The Foothills Trail continues along the west bank, but this ride turns around here and heads back to the parking area.

This area, known as "the Horsepasture," is rich in history. The lower Cherokee Nation's center was just south of Lake Jocassee. Many Indian artifacts and remains have been discovered in this area. The name of this flat bottom land is believed to have come from the natural horse corral formed by the steep slopes leading away from the confluence of the Horsepasture, Toxaway, and Laurel Fork rivers.

0.0   From the pull-off on Frozen Creek Road, begin cycling the dirt road.

0.3 Bear right at the fork in the road. You will pass several houses in this area.

0.5 There is a trail on the left; continue straight. Frozen Lake is on the left.

0.9 There is a trail on the right; continue straight.

4.2 Toxaway Creek is on the left.

4.5 The Foothills Trail bleeds into the dirt road from the left. You will cross the Toxaway River on a suspension bridge.

5.1 You will arrive at Cane Brake. You may want to linger here to enjoy the views of Lake Jocassee before turning around and retracing your path.

10.2 You will arrive back at Frozen Creek Road.

Gently flowing creek along the trail

Index

Notes

Notes

Notes

Notes

Notes

Notes

Notes